English for Accounting

Evan Frendo · Sean Mahoney

SHORT COURSE
SERIES

Verfasser	Evan Frendo, Berlin
	Sean Mahoney, Berlin
Verlagsredaktion	Janan Barksdale
Redaktionelle Mitarbeit	Christine House, Fritz Preuss (Wortliste), Ellie Robertson
Umschlaggestaltung/Layout	Sylvia Lang
Bildredaktion	Gertha Maly

Bildquellen

Fotos: Getty/Anne Rippy S.5; Getty/Paul King S.10; Comstock (1. und 3. Foto), Corbis/Jim Craigmyle (Foto Mitte) S.12; Comstock S.14; Getty/B&M Productions S.18; Comstock S.20; Corbis/Chris Carroll S.21; Getty/Reza Estakhrian S.21; Corbis S.21; Comstock (2 Fotos), Getty/Tim Brown S.22; Corbis/Jim Craigmyle S.26; Corbis/Paul Barton S.26; Corbis/Helen King S.30; Corbis/Fotografia S.32; Getty/White Packert S.33; Comstock S.35; Getty/S.39; Getty/Phil Boorman S.42; Getty/S.44; Corbis/Jose Luis Pelaez S.45

Cartoons: Oxford Designers & Illustrators

Nicht alle Copyright-Inhaber konnten ermittelt werden, deren Urheberrechte werden hiermit vorsorglich und ausdrücklich anerkannt.

Weitere Titel in der *Short Course Series*:
English for Emails Bestell.-Nr. 18784
English for the Automobile Industry Bestell.-Nr. 18776

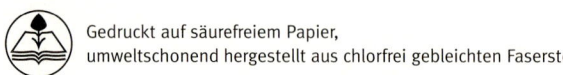 http://www.cornelsen.de

1. Auflage   Druck 4 3 2 1   Jahr 06 05 04 03

Alle Drucke dieser Auflage sind inhaltlich unverändert
und können im Unterricht nebeneinander verwendet werden.

Druck: CS-Druck CornelsenStürtz, Berlin

ISBN 3-464-01880-6

Bestellnummer 18806

Gedruckt auf säurefreiem Papier,
umweltschonend hergestellt aus chlorfrei gebleichten Faserstoffen.

Contents

PAGE	UNIT TITLE	TOPICS	USEFUL LANGUAGE AND SKILLS
5	**1 Introduction to accounting**	Jobs in accounting Accounting principles Creative accounting CPA & Chartered Accountant	Meeting people Offering hospitality Agreeing and disagreeing
14	**2 Financial statements and ratios**	Profit and Loss Statement Balance Sheet Explaining accounts Ratio analysis	Saying numbers in English Saying formulas/equations Making comparisons
22	**3 Tax Accounting**	Tax systems Methods of depreciation Calculating tax expense Taxation planning	Clarifying information Being polite
29	**4 Auditing**	Role of auditors Types of audits Auditor-client relationship Describing graphs An auditor's report	Telephone phrases Making appointments Talking about trends Talking about causes and results
35	**5 Management accounting**	Defining management accounting Statement of Cash Flows Budgets The future of accounting	Meeting phrases
42	**6 Investment**	Cross-border investments Different accounting practices Intercultural issues Globalization and the role of accountants	Presentation phrases Organizing a presentation

PAGE	APPENDIX
48	**Test yourself!**
	Partner file
50	Partner A
52	Partner B
54	**Answer key**
58	**A–Z wordlist**
62	**Glossary of financial terms**
64	**Useful phrases and vocabulary**

Vorwort

English for Accounting wurde speziell für Leute entwickelt, die in dem Bereich Rechnungswesen und Finanzen tätig sind und die nötigen Englischkenntnisse brauchen, um in verschiedensten Situationen mit Kollegen und Geschäftspartnern zu kommunizieren. Ob bei Meetings oder Präsentationen, am Telefon oder beim Smalltalk, mit diesem SHORT COURSE können Sie gezielt notwendige Redewendungen und Wortschatz erlernen um Ihre geschäftliche Ziele zu erreichen.

English for Accounting besteht aus sechs Units, die unterschiedliche Gebiete des Rechnungswesens behandeln. Jede Unit beginnt mit dem sogenannten **Start-up**, das aus kurzen Übungen, *Brainstorming* oder einem Quiz besteht. Daraufhin folgen Dialoge, Texte und authentische Dokumente sowie ein Vielfalt von Übungen, die helfen, wichtige Vokabeln und Redewendungen im Kontext zu erlernen. Es gibt in den Units Verweisstellen auf die **Partner files** im Anhang – *Information-gap*-Übungen in Form von Rollenspielen, die Ihnen die Möglichkeit geben, in typischen Situationen den gelernten Wortschatz der Unit mit einem Partner oder einer Partnerin zu trainieren.

In **English for Accounting** geht es nicht nur um aktives Sprechen, es werden auch Fachthemen behandelt. Am Ende jeder Unit finden Sie einen **Optional reading**-Text, dessen Inhalt sich auf das Thema der Unit bezieht und zur Diskussion anregt. Darüberhinaus vermitteln **Did you know?**-Kästchen landeskundliche und sprachliche Informationen zum Rechnungswesen bzw. zum allgemeinen Berufsleben in englischsprachigen Ländern.

Wenn Sie mit den Units fertig sind, haben Sie die Möglichkeit Ihre Kenntnisse mit einem Kreuzworträtsel zu überprüfen, in dem das Vokabular des SHORT COURSE wiederholt wird – **Test yourself!**

Im Anhang von **English for Accounting** finden Sie einen **Answer Key**, mit dem Sie Ihre Lösungen selbstständig überprüfen können. Der Anhang enthält außerdem eine hilfreiche **A–Z wordlist**, ein **Glossary of financial terms** sowie eine kompakte Zusammenfassung von **Useful phrases and vocabulary**, so dass Sie auch am Arbeitsplatz die gebräuchlichsten Fachbegriffe sowie Redewendungen schnell nachschlagen können.

Introduction to accounting

Make a list of all the different types of jobs you know about in accounting.

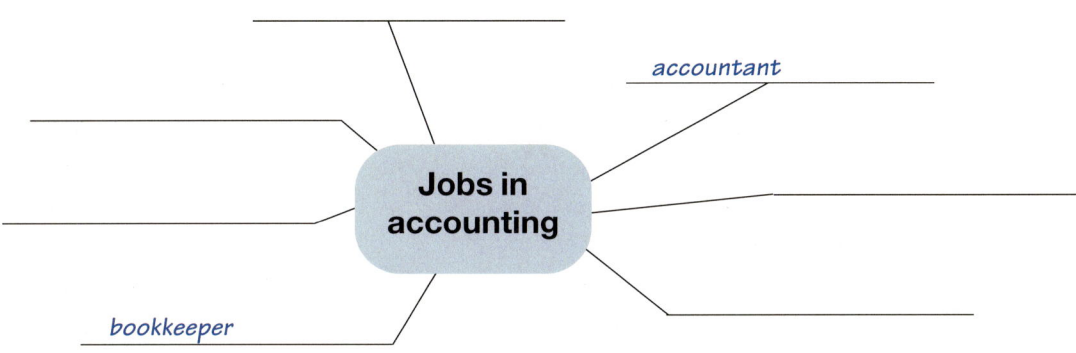

accountant

Jobs in accounting

bookkeeper

1 **Michael Rogers, a CPA (Certified Public Accountant) from the US, is meeting Hans Senkel, the CFO (Chief Financial Officer) of a company in Frankfurt. What is the reason for the meeting? Are there any jobs mentioned which are not in your list?**

Secretary	Mr Senkel will be with you in a moment. He's just finishing a phone call.
Michael	Thank you.
Secretary	Would you like some coffee?
Michael	Yes, that would be great. Black, please.
Secretary	Here you are.
Michael	Thank you.
Michael	Is this the whole department?
Secretary	No, no, not at all. On this floor we have the accountants and the bookkeepers.
Michael	Uh-huh.
Secretary	Downstairs are the internal auditors. And at the moment we have a team of external auditors. They're in one of the conference rooms at the end of the corridor.
Michael	I see.
Secretary	Ah, Herr Senkel. This is Michael Rogers.

Hans	Ah, yes. Hello, Michael. I'm Hans. It's nice to meet you. Sorry to keep you waiting. Please come in and take a seat. Did you have a nice flight?
Michael	Yes, thanks, Hans. Finding the office was a little more difficult, though. I'm glad so many people here in Frankfurt can speak English.

Hans	Oh yes, we're fairly international here now. But that's not a bad thing, I must say.
Michael	A little cultural mix is good, isn't it?
Hans	You're absolutely right. Would you like to start by telling me a little about your experience, Michael? Your resumé is very impressive. And then I'll fill you in on our group, and the particular requirements we have for this position.
Michael	Yes, that's fine. I guess you know from my resumé that I studied economics in Paris, ...

2 **Here are some mixed-up phrases from the conversation. Re-order them so that they make sense.**

1 in Mr moment Senkel you with will be a.
2 have Did you a flight nice?
3 coffee Would some you like?
4 keep Sorry you to waiting.

5 come Please in seat take and a.
6 call finishing He's just phone a.
7 to nice you meet It's.

3 **Fill in the gaps with a suitable word from the box.**

bad • absolutely • very • know • start • fill • fairly

1 You're _____ right.

2 Would you like to _____ by telling me a little about your experience?

3 I guess you _____ that I studied economics in Paris.

4 And then I'll _____ you in on our group.

5 Your resumé is _____ impressive.

6 But that's not a _____ thing.

7 We're _____ international here now.

4 **Make two lists. In the first, write down topics which would be safe to talk about with a foreign business partner. In the second, write down unsafe topics. Compare with a partner.**

Safe topics

Unsafe topics

5   **Work with a partner to practise greetings and small talk. Look at the phrases in the box before you go to the partner file.**

PARTNER FILE   Partner A   page 50
Partner B   page 52

USEFUL PHRASES

Meeting people
Hello, Mr/Ms … . I'm … .
It's nice to meet you.
– (It's) Nice to meet you, too.
May I introduce you to … ?
I'd like to introduce you to … .
Have you met … ?

Offering hospitality
Can I take your coat?
Please come in and take a seat.
Can I get you a cup of coffee/tea?
Would you like something to drink?
– Yes, please./Yes, that would be great.
– No, thank you./No, thanks.

6   **What do the following abbreviations mean? Check your answers in the article below.**

GAAP • IFRS • IAS • IASC

International accounting

International companies can choose how they present financial information to outside parties. The rules and regulations between countries vary significantly. Accountants worldwide are familiar with the words "Generally Accepted Accounting Principles (GAAP)". Some of the basic principles are:

■ the going concern principle
■ the prudence principle
■ the matching principle
■ the consistency principle

The development of these principles has greatly differed between countries. For example, in most English-speaking countries it is often accepted practice to offset unrealized gains from unrealized losses, or to re-value long term assets upwards, provided sufficient proof of the current value can be shown. This means that accounts can have very different values, depending on whether the company chooses to follow local accounting standards, International Financial Reporting Standards (IFRS) – formerly the International Accounting Standards (IAS)– or US GAAP Whether the company can choose is governed by the laws of the country where it is registered. For example, the USA and Japan currently allow publicly-traded companies to prepare their financial statements using the standards of the International Accounting Standards Committee (IASC), but they must also include a reconciliation to domestic GAAP.

VOCABULARY ASSISTANT

currently *zurzeit*   domestic *inländisch*   to govern *bestimmen*
provided *vorausgesetzt*   reconciliation *Abstimmung*

7 **Use words from each box to make word partnerships. Then match them to the definitions below.**

> outside • accepted • English-speaking • local accounting • publicly-traded

> company • practice • standards • parties • countries

1 A firm that sells its shares to anyone who wants to buy them.
2 For example, Australia, the UK and the USA.
3 The way that most people do something.
4 The rules and regulations which state how accountants operate in a particular place.
5 People or groups who are not involved with the company.

8 **The article mentions four basic principles of accounting. Match them to the definitions below. Then check your answers in the glossary (→ page 62).**

1 [   ]

This principle is concerned with the timing of the recognition of transactions in the accounts. Items are recorded when the income or expense arises, and are not dependent on the movement of cash.

2 [   ]

When preparing accounts, one must assume that the enterprise will still be viable in the years to come. Practically all accounting items are affected by this assumption, such as the carrying value of fixed assets and inventories, and the ability to repay debts and other obligations.

3 [   ]

What value should be given to the numbers in the accounts? It is normal to act pessimistically, so that profits and assets are not overstated, and expenses and liabilities realistically valued.

4 [   ]

Accounts should be produced using the same principles from one year to the next. Deviations from this principle must be noted, and the effects on the accounts shown.

9 **Do you know of any differences in the application of these principles between countries? What should a visiting accountant know about the principles in your country? Make notes, and prepare to brief someone else in the class.**

10 **True or false? Read this email on creative accounting, and then check the statements at the end.**

Delete Reply Reply All Forward Print

Subject: Creative accounting
From: Rupert Greene <r.greene@intep.de>
To: Johannes Bauer <j.bauer@intep.de>

Hi Johannes

At our meeting yesterday you asked me to send you some background info on 'creative accounting', and in particular 'off-balance-sheet accounting'.

Basically there's quite a bit of flexibility in the way we can interpret the standards and principles of accounting. For example, we may want to report bigger profits so that we can attract investors on the capital markets. On the other hand, smaller profits may be better so that we pay less tax. The problem is that the line between truthful and misleading representation of figures is sometimes very thin, and this is where people get into trouble.

'Off-balance-sheet accounting' is seen by some as one type of creative accounting. (People have been arguing about it for years, though!) The key point to remember is that the accounting treatment of legitimate business transactions can vary greatly. For example, many companies are involved in leasing for business reasons, and the question for the accountants is how to present the financial implications of such leases in the accounts. In theory, the idea is that leasing an asset (instead of buying it) allows the company to exclude the liability from its accounts.

Hope this helps – give me a call if you have any more questions.

Best wishes

Rupert

VOCABULARY ASSISTANT
to exclude *ausschließen* implication *Auswirkung*
legitimate *berechtigt* misleading *irreführend*

1 Accountants agree that creative accounting is a good thing. ❑
2 'Off-balance-sheet accounting' is one way of 'creative accounting' – there are others. ❑
3 Creative accounting is sometimes used to try and attract more investors. ❑
4 Accountants are allowed some flexibility in the way they present accounts. ❑
5 Leasing is actually illegal. ❑
6 Big profits mean paying less tax. ❑
7 When a company leases an asset, the accountant doesn't have to include it in the accounts. ❑

11 **Read the following dialogue between the Managing Director (Charles) and the Financial Director (Sabine) of an organization which is investing in a new factory near Hanover. Do you think they share the same opinion about creative accounting?**

Sabine	Morning Charles. You wanted to see me?
Charles	Yeah. Hi Sabine. About our board meeting next week, you know we'll be discussing our debt problems?
Sabine	Of course. Probably our biggest issue at the moment.
Charles	Right. The shareholders are getting nervous, and the markets don't like our level of gearing. We're getting more and more questions about whether we can service our debt, in the long term. It's getting harder to

attract new investments. So I wanted to speak to you about what we can do. Our new factory near Dresden is very important, and we're looking at leasing the assets. And that's where you come in. Tell me what we can do with leases on the balance sheet. What's allowed in this country?

Sabine	Is this a business decision, to lease these assets?
Charles	Let's just say it's one possibility we're looking at.
Sabine	You're thinking that if we lease the assets, we can exclude these liabilities from the balance sheet?
Charles	Exactly.
Sabine	You know that the auditors will look very closely at these transactions? The accounting standards, or principles if you like, mean that finance leases must be disclosed. If we are effectively the owner of these assets, then we're not going to have a choice.
Charles	And how do we determine the owner?
Sabine	That depends on the conditions in the contract.
Charles	That shouldn't be a problem. And then we can call them …
Sabine	Operating leases. But remember, auditors and the markets are now very sensitive to these things. We can't afford to be seen as trying to mislead anyone.
Charles	Of course not. But for the meeting next week, have a think about it. OK?
Sabine	Yeah. I'll try and bring some ideas.
Charles	Great. See you later.
Sabine	OK. Bye.

DID YOU KNOW?

Accounting bodies and regulators now look at creative accounting issues very closely. The International Accounting Standards Committee designed its 'Standard on Leasing Contracts' (or IAS 17) to recognize the substance of lease contracts, and not only their legal form. By requiring that financial statements give a true and fair representation of an organization's performance and financial position, the standard enables people reading these statements to make fully informed decisions.

12 **Match these words with their meanings.**

1	debt	a	an agreement between two or more parties, often written
2	lease	b	the opposite of assets
3	gearing	c	buying or selling something
4	liabilities	d	someone who owns parts of a company
5	contract	e	money that is owed
6	transaction	f	an agreement where the owner of something allows someone else to use it for a specific time for a sum of money
7	shareholder	g	the proportion of own capital to borrowed funds when buying an asset or financing a company

DID YOU KNOW?

Two of these words (liability and debt) have almost the same meaning, yet can be used quite differently.

Liability (*Verpflichtung*) means that there is an obligation to pay. Note that in insurance, liability normally refers to risk and responsibility; an example of this is deciding who pays the costs of an accident. In accounting, liability normally refers to an expense or a loan. It is often seen as a balance sheet item. In this sense liabilities are the opposite of assets. A debt (*Schuld*) is a form of liability.

13 **Use liability, liabilities, debt or debts to complete the sentences below.**

1 He'll have paid his _____ off by next year.

2 Look at the assets and _____ on the balance sheet if you want to know how the company's doing.

3 Many Third World countries are burdened by heavy _____.

4 We need to look at the long term _____ before we think about any major new purchases.

5 The partnership has limited _____ status.

6 Current _____ are those which are paid off within a year.

7 The company's in _____ to the tune of 10 million.

I'VE BALANCED THE BOOKS – NOW ASSETS EQUAL LIABILITIES!

MD

14 In the conversation in exercise 11, Sabine agrees with Charles. Here are some other ways to agree or disagree with someone. Put a tick (✔) next to the ones which mean agreement, and a cross (✗) next to those which mean disagreement.

1 You've got a point there. ☐
2 I see what you mean. ☐
3 Me neither. ☐
4 No way. ☐

5 It's just not on. ☐
6 Fair enough. ☐
7 Point taken. ☐

15 Now use the above expressions to respond to the following statements. Note that more than one answer is possible.

1 "I think we should work fewer hours. I mean, almost everyone else in this company now works 35-hour weeks, and look at us!" "_____"

2 "Can you come in next weekend?" "What again? _____"

3 "I'd like you to prepare the figures for next week's presentation. But this time could you make sure that you put our current client's name on the slides." "_____"

4 "We need to finish this by next Wednesday. How about if we postpone the department party? There's no other way." "_____"

5 "Have you had a look at this? It's a disaster, a catastrophe!" "Hang on, it can't be that bad. Ah, _____"

6 "Look, we really need to convince the boss that some of the transactions have been wrongly booked. I don't want problems later." "_____"

7 "They want us to take a pay cut this year." "Are you kidding? _____"

16 Do you agree with the speaker? Use the phrases above to agree or disagree and continue the discussion with a partner.

Off balance sheet accounting should be made illegal.

Creative accounting is a good thing.

It's time the world moved to the same accounting principles – everyone should use US GAAP.

OPTIONAL READING

Becoming an accountant

CPA

The body which represents the interests of accountants in the US is the American Institute of Certified Public Accountants (AICPA). To become a CPA, the applicant must meet the requirements of the state where he/she wishes to practise, as established by the law of that state and administered by the state boards of accountancy.
To qualify for certification, the applicant must:

1   study accountancy at a college or university
2   pass the CPA examination, which consists of four sections:
    • Business Law and Professional Responsibilities
    • Auditing
    • Accounting and Reporting-Taxation, Managerial, and Governmental and Not-for-Profit Organizations
    • Financial Accounting and Reporting – Business Enterprises
3   have professional work experience in public accounting.

Most states require a qualified CPA to carry out regular professional training.

Chartered accountant

The major accounting body in the UK is the Institute of Chartered Accountants in England and Wales (ICAEW).
To become a Chartered Accountant, the applicant must:

1   have sufficient school or university education
2   apply for a training contract with a recognized company, which will give him/her three years work experience
3   pass the ICAEW's exams on:
    • Accounting
    • Audit and Assurance
    • Business Finance
    • Business Management
    • Financial Reporting
    • Taxation
4   as well as prove his/her knowledge on Commercial and Company Law, and then with further exams on:
    • Business Environment
    • Business Life Cycle
    • Advanced Case Study

Over to you

How does the process of becoming an accountant in your country compare to those described above?
Describe the general accounting rules and practices in your country. What standards are used to prepare financial information? How is off-balance-sheet accounting treated in your country? How is leasing reported in accounts?

2 Financial statements and ratios

Balance Sheet, Statement of Cash Flows, Statement of Earnings ...

Statement of Financial Position, Notes, Annual Report, Budget ...

Market Capitalization, Discounted Cash Flows ...

Management Accounts, Investments, Statement of Shareholder's Equity ...

The man in the picture is thinking about different types of financial statements. Which ones are you familiar with? Can you explain what they are used for?

1 Here are two typical examples of the disclosures required under US law.
In the UK one would be called a 'Balance Sheet', and the other a 'Profit and Loss Statement'.
In the US they have other names. Which is which?

Statement of Financial Position

At December 31 (In millions)	2002	2001
Assets		
Cash and equivalents	$ 13,485	$ 18,278
Investment securities	67,833	61,890
Current receivables	7,290	6,870
Inventories	3,444	3,281
Financing receivables	121,189	113,871
Insurance receivables	2,560	2,187
Other receivables	985	1,009
Property, plant and equipment – net	46,005	44,875
Investments	18,320	18,320
Intangible assets	19,836	17,998
All other assets	65,871	62,755
Total assets	**$ 366,818**	**$ 351,334**
Liabilities and equity		
Short-term borrowings	$ 95,531	92,736
Accounts payable	12,894	10,209
Progress collections	2,890	3,897
Dividends payable	1,155	1,102
All other current costs and expenses accrued	9,598	8,293
Long-term borrowings	75,728	70,354
Insurance liabilities, reserves and annuity benefits	85,389	84,283
All other liabilities	37,487	33,763
Deferred income taxes	12,736	14,198
Total Liabilities	**333,408**	**318,835**

Minority interest in equity of consolidated affiliates	2,374	2,179
Common stock	1,214	1,214
Accumulated gains/(losses) – net	2,189	2,427
Other capital	9,827	9,834
Retained earnings	30,545	29,772
Less common stock held in treasury	(12,739)	(12,927)
Total share owners equity	31,036	30,320
Total liabilities and equity	$ 366,818	$ 351,334

Statement of Earnings

For the years ended December 31 (In millions; per share amounts in dollars)	2002	2001	2000
Revenues			
Sales of goods	$ 80,746	$ 78,847	$ 74,387
Sales of services	4,384	4,267	5,925
Other income	1,212	1,434	1,228
Total revenues	86,342	84,548	81,540
Costs and expenses			
Cost of goods sold	28,659	27,498	25,728
Cost of services sold	4,112	4,255	5,601
Interest and financial charges	8,518	8,855	8,645
Insurance losses and policyholder and annuity benefits	10,372	10,137	9,928
Provision for losses on financing receivables	4,374	4,561	4,612
Other costs and expenses	16,811	16,735	14,480
Minority interest in net earnings of consolidated affiliates	215	188	195
Total costs and expenses	73,061	72,229	69,189
Earnings before income taxes and accounting changes	13,281	12,319	12,351
Provision for income taxes	(3,547)	(3,188)	(3,441)
Earnings before accounting changes	9,734	9,131	8,910
Cumulative effect of accounting changes	0	(212)	0
Net earnings	$ 9,734	$ 8,919	$ 8,910
Per-share amounts			
Per-share amounts before accounting changes			
Diluted earnings per share	$ 1.22	$ 1.16	$ 1.13
Basic earnings per share	$ 1.23	$ 1.17	$ 1.14
Per-share amounts after accounting changes			
Diluted earnings per share	$ 1.22	$ 1.13	$ 1.13
Basic earnings per share	$ 1.23	$ 1.14	$ 1.14
Dividends declared per share	$ 0.49	$ .046	$ 0.45

2   Match the words with their partners, and then look at the statements again to check.

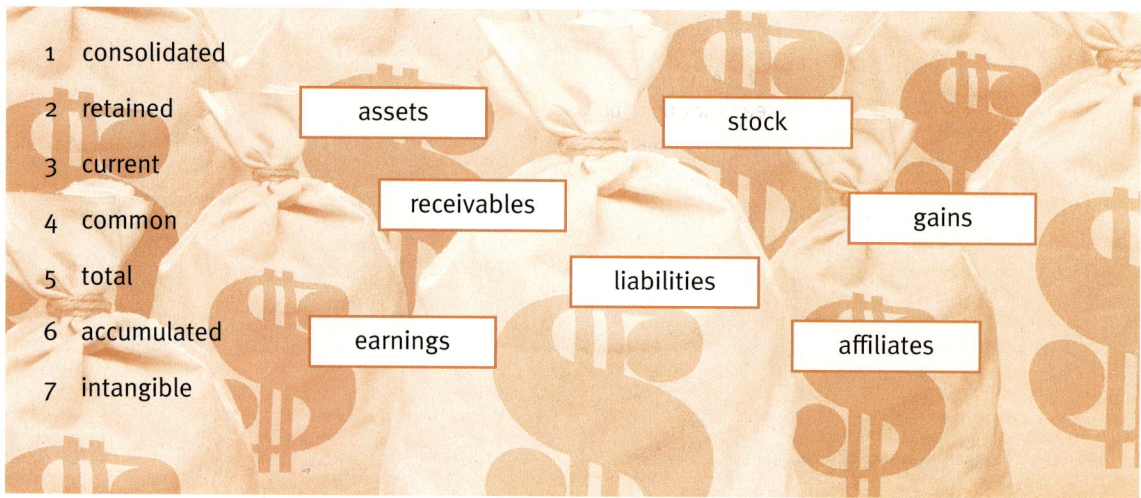

1   consolidated

2   retained

3   current

4   common

5   total

6   accumulated

7   intangible

assets

stock

receivables

gains

liabilities

earnings

affiliates

Now match the word partners to their definitions.

a   An asset which does not have a physical nature (such as a trademark or a patent).

b   The holding company owns a minority interest (less than 50%), but the accounts are nevertheless consolidated.

c   The total legal obligations of a company to pay other parties.

d   The ordinary shares held by the owners, who therefore are the last to receive their money back in the event of liquidation.

e   Amounts that will be collected in the normal course of business within one year.

f   Profit which is not paid out to shareholders in the form of dividends, but instead is kept by the company to reinvest or pay off debts.

g   The amounts affecting common stockholders, but not from movements in the stock of the company (eg currency translation adjustments).

3   Compare the financial statements on pages 14 and 15 to ones from your country. Make some notes for a colleague in the US, summarizing the major differences in the layout.

DID YOU KNOW?

The UK and the USA often have different terms for the same thing. Here are some important examples. Can you think of any others?

UK	USA	German
Balance Sheet	Statement of Financial Position	*Bilanz*
Profit and Loss Statement	Statement of Earnings	*Gewinn und Verlust Rechnung (GuV)*
shareholder	stockholder	*Aktionär/in*
stock	inventory	*Waren- oder Lagerbestand*
gearing	leverage	*Fremdkapitalaufnahme*

4 **Choose the best way to say these numbers and equations. (Sometimes more than one way is possible.)**

23.56
a twenty-three comma fifty-six
b twenty-three point fifty-six
c twenty-three point five six
d two three point five six

1999
a nineteen ninety-nine
b nineteen hundred ninety-nine
c nineteen nine nine
d one nine nine nine

10,001
a one thousand and one
b ten thousand one
c ten thousand and one
d one triple oh one

2003
a two thousand three
b two double oh three
c two thousand and three
d twenty oh three

£63.30
a sixty-three pound and thirty pence
b sixty-three pounds and thirty pence
c sixty-three pounds and thirteen pence
d sixty-three pounds thirty

5,400,342
a five hundred thousand, four hundred, three hundred and forty-two
b five million, four hundred thousand, three hundred and twenty-four
c five million, four hundred thousand, three hundred and forty-two
d five billion, four hundred thousand, three hundred and twenty-four

€45,638
a forty-five thousand, six hundred and thirty-eight euros
b forty-five thousand, six hundred and eighty-three euros
c forty-five thousand, six hundred and three eight euros
d forty-five, sixty-three, eight euros

DID YOU KNOW?

Saying numbers in English

Notice how we use the decimal point in English:

6.02 six point oh two
0.04 zero (or nought) point oh four
0.007 zero point double oh seven
56.345 fifty-six point three four five [NB: single numbers after the decimal!]

Here commas – and not decimal points – are used:

12,076 twelve thousand and seventy-six
2,534,210 two million, five hundred and thirty-four thousand, two hundred and ten

Note the following:

1,000,000 one million
1,000,000,000 one billion

Sums of money:

€3.67 three euro**s** sixty-seven
(NOT: ~~three euro sixty-seven~~)
$5 m five million dollar**s**

Note how we say years:

1987 nineteen eighty-seven
2003 two thousand and three
2030 two thousand and thirty (or twenty thirty)

5 **Work with a partner to check on some figures. Use the information in your partner file to make a phone call.**

PARTNER FILE   Partner A   page 50   Partner B   page 52

6 **We often make comparisons when talking about financial statements. Look again at the statement of earnings on page 15 and find the figures for the items below. Which sentences (a–h) can be used to describe and compare the figures?**

1 Net earnings
2 Interest and financial charges
3 Basic earnings per share (2000 and 2001)
4 Earnings before income taxes and accounting changes

5 Total revenues
6 Dividends declared per share
7 Other costs and expenses
8 Sales of services

a It's better than last year.

c There's quite a drop from 2000 to 2001.

d It's not as low as two years ago.

b It's gone down since last year.

g It's virtually the same.

f A lot more this year.

e Slightly more this year.

h It's exactly the same.

7 **Ratio analysis is a quantitative approach which can be used to analyse the performance of a company. Here an American accountant explains some of the key ratios to some German managers. Make a list of typical ratios you are familiar with, and then compare your ratios to those mentioned in the conversation.**

Accountant OK. Norma has asked me to go over some of the ratios I used in the report which I sent you last week. The first of these is on page 3 – 'working capital'. Everyone got it? OK. Working capital is quite simple – it's the current assets divided by the current liabilities. Question, Hans?

Hans What's it for?

Accountant Well, it basically tells us whether we have enough short term assets to cover our short term debt. If we don't, we could be in trouble. OK? Good. Next is 'return on assets'. This is net income plus interest expense divided by total assets. Before you ask, it allows us to evaluate the way we use our assets. It can help us decide whether or not we should start a new project, for example, by comparing the return expected against the normal borrowing costs. Is that clear?

Heike I have a question. What's debt/asset ratio?

Accountant I was just coming to that. It's the total assets divided by total liabilities. It tells us what proportion of the enterprise's assets are being financed through the use of debt. If this ratio is high in a market with increasing interest rates, creditors are going to get worried. The debt/asset ratio determines the funding leverage of the enterprise. OK, if there are no questions, I'd like to …

Working

capital =

Saying equations/formulas

+	plus, and, add	
−	minus, less, subtract	
÷	divided by	
—	divided by, over	
x	multiplied by, times	
=	equals, is	

$a \times b = c$ a times (or multiplied by) b equals c

$\dfrac{a - b}{c}$ a minus b divided by (or over) c

$\dfrac{\text{total assets}}{\text{total liabilities}}$ total assets divided by total liabilities

8   **Some other common ratios are given below. Match the ratios with the formulas (1–7) and the descriptions (a–g).**

> gross profit margin • earnings per share • return on equity • average interest rate • debt/equity ratio • inventory turnover • price/earnings ratio

1   $\dfrac{\text{interest expenses} - \text{accounts payable}}{\text{liabilities}}$

2   $\dfrac{\text{net income} - \text{dividends on preferred stock}}{\text{average shares}}$

3   $\dfrac{\text{net income}}{\text{shareholder's equity}}$

4   $\dfrac{\text{total liabilities}}{\text{shareholder's equity}}$

5   $\dfrac{\text{revenue} - \text{cost of goods sold}}{\text{revenue}}$

6   $\dfrac{\text{cost of goods sold}}{\text{average inventory}}$

7   $\dfrac{\text{market value per share}}{\text{earnings per share}}$

a   Gives the company's pricing policy and mark-up margins. An adequate gross margin allows a company to pay its expenses, and then expand.

b   Determines the average interest rate at which a company borrows funds.

c   Compares the current market price with earnings to calculate if a stock is over or under valued. Used as a prediction or expectation of future performance.

d   Indicates the return a company gets on the owners' investment. Companies that make high returns often do not require more debt investments.

e   Shows the turnover of inventory, and can be compared against sales figures, to show the demand for the company's products.

f   Indicates what proportion of equity and debt an enterprise uses to finance its assets. A more stringent test is to use just the long term debt.

g   Calculates the profit made on a per share basis. This is quoted by US publicly held companies in their financial statements.

VOCABULARY ASSISTANT   average *durchschnittlich*   inventory *Waren- oder Lagerbestand*   prediction *Vorhersage*   proportion *Anteil*   stringent *zwingend*

9   **Use words from the descriptions above to complete the table. The first one is done for you.**

VERB	NOUN
to predict	prediction
to _____ 1	payment
to _____ 2	comparison
to _____ 3	calculation
to expect	_____ 4
to _____ 5	indication
to _____ 6	expansion
to perform	_____ 7

Now use verbs or nouns from above to complete the sentences. You may need to change the form.

a   The figures are a little different to what we were _____.

b   The problems in the Middle East have made it really difficult to _____ next year's turnover.

c   I think there are some mistakes in the _____.

d   The fund _____ much better last year. This year has been very disappointing.

e   The _____ into Eastern Europe looks good.

f   We need to make sure that our customers _____ us on time.

10   **Here are some phrases the accountant uses during the meeting. Can you fill in the missing words?**

questions • just • that • got • over • ask

1   Norma has asked me to go _____ some of the ratios I used in my report

2   I was _____ coming to that.

3   Before you _____ ...

4   Everyone _____ it?

5   OK, if there are no _____ , I'd like to ...

6   Is _____ clear?

11   **Calculate the working capital, earnings per share and the inventory turnover of the company at the start of the chapter (for 2001 and 2002), and then compare your results with a partner's. Discuss possible reasons for the changes.**

OPTIONAL READING

Read what these people say about financial statements. Which comments do you agree with? How would you respond to the people you don't agree with?

Accountant: The financial statements of a company are the most important documents that a company produces. Investors, creditors, banks, customers – everybody reads the statements. The accounts show what a company does with its money, how profitable it is, and also how risk-worthy it is. And you can see warning signs for the future. Our stock exchanges depend on properly prepared accounts.

Trader: I agree that the accounts of the companies have a lot of information, but it's very hard to understand it all. In my job, I need to know the financial situation of a company. People interested in the stock exchanges rely on experts like me. But there are also many other sources of information. As for the accounting rules, they don't interest me, or anyone else, at all. That's stuff for the accountants.

Investor: All those numbers, and I haven't got a clue what they all mean. Pages and pages of them, and apparently they are often only 'estimates', or they can be interpreted in one of many ways. What's the point when the accountants themselves can't agree on how to show the numbers? Most of us need a lot more information and knowledge about a company than what we get in the accounts.

Layman: Is it all really that hard? Can't we just look at the profit or loss of the company to find out how it's doing? I don't see all the fuss. Accountants are there to tell us about the numbers, and I thought that's what they do. They are trained to report these numbers, and it can't be that hard to count up everything that's happened.

Managing Director: This is exactly the problem. There are many ways to change the numbers to give a better picture. Some of my peers have been guilty of doing just that. The accountants and auditors have to take responsibility for the way that numbers are reported. Accountants and their work are extremely important, they just need to make it all a little easier to understand.

Over to You

In your experience, what do people think of the work done by accountants? What do they generally think about financial statements?

How can accountants make the numbers they produce easier to understand?

3 Tax accounting

There are some types of tax in the boxes below, but some letters are missing. Can you complete the words?

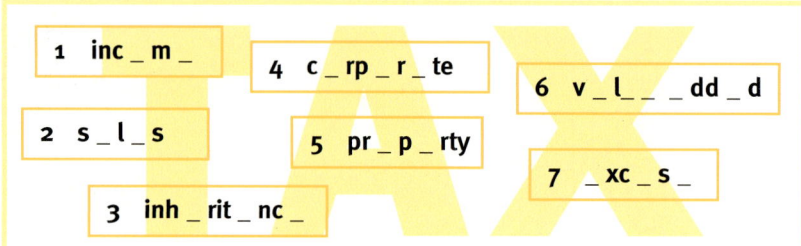

1 inc _ m _

2 s _ l _ s

3 inh _ rit _ nc _

4 c _ rp _ r _ te

5 pr _ p _ rty

6 v _ l _ _ _ dd _ d

7 _ xc _ s _

Which taxes in the boxes above are you familiar with?
What do foreign companies and individuals need to know about the taxation system in your country?

1 A German manager has asked his accountant to explain depreciation. First make a list of some typical methods. Then read the following conversation. Are the same methods given?

Uwe So could you just go over depreciation again?

Jill Sure. I've prepared a quick list of the different types like you asked.

Uwe Great.

Jill OK, let's see. Well, you know that the normal accounting treatment means that a fixed asset has to be written off over its useful life. Basically we look at the cost of the item, and take away its estimated scrap value. Then we use a depreciation method to write it off.

Uwe Yes, of course. It's five years for computers, I think.

Jill Right. Well, as you say, there are different ways of doing this. Er, let's see, straight line, declining balance, sum-of-the-years'-digits, unit of production, hours of use. If you look at this list, you can see a description of each of these methods.

Uwe Oh yes, I see. Yes, that's very useful.

Jill OK. Let's start with straight line ...

VOCABULARY ASSISTANT	depreciation *Abschreibung* scrap value *Schrottwert* to write off *abschreiben*

DID YOU KNOW?

In the US and Britain accounting methods for income tax and financial reporting are independent of each other. This means that there can be large differences between the profit recorded in the financial statements and the profit for the income tax calculation.

2   **Now look at Jill's list of definitions. Can you match them to the methods of depreciation she mentions?**

1   _____: The asset is depreciated by a constant amount every year. The depreciation expense for each year is calculated by subtracting the salvage value from the acquisition cost, and then dividing the difference by the useful life of the asset.

2   _____: The depreciation expense is calculated by first subtracting the salvage value from the acquisition cost. The difference is multiplied by a fractional amount, where the denominator and numerator are based on the addition of the figures in the asset's useful life.

3   _____: The depreciation is 'accelerated' by this method, so that the expense is greater in the first years. The salvage value is ignored in the calculation, but the asset will not be depreciated below this value.

4   _____: The expected usage of the asset is taken into account in determining the rate of depreciation.

5   _____: The expected output of the asset is taken into account in determining the rate of depreciation.

VOCABULARY ASSISTANT   accelerated *beschleunigt*   denominator *Nenner*   fractional amount *Bruchteil*
numerator *Zähler*   salvage value *Bergungswert*   to take into account *berücksichtigen*

3   **Prepare a short presentation on depreciation methods. First read the questions below and note down your answers. Then organize your notes and give your presentation.**

- What depreciation method does your company/client use on its assets?
- Why has your company/client chosen that method?
- What are the alternatives in your country for depreciating assets?

4 **An accountant explains the taxation expense disclosure requirements to a CEO.**
Read the dialogue and complete the CEO's notes.

> Taxation expense is calculated by subtracting _____
> _____ ¹ from _____ ²
> This gives us an estimate, which we use to _____
> _____ ³
> We need it to justify _____ ⁴
> If there is any difference between the profit before tax and the
> taxable income, we _____
> _____ ⁵

CEO	We've got a few minutes to ourselves. Could you just go over it again? How is the taxation expense calculated?
Accountant	OK. The operating profit minus our interest expenses gives us the profit before tax figure. This is the amount which theoretically is then subject to taxation. In fact, the taxation amount is just an estimate, because we won't know until much later exactly how much tax we will have to pay.
CEO	What do we do with this estimate?
Accountant	In effect, we prepare an interim tax return. It won't be filed, just kept by us to justify the taxation expense we include in the P&L.
CEO	Will this also be audited?
Accountant	Yes. And of course, the profit after tax is the figure which we can distribute to shareholders.
CEO	What do we do when the taxable income differs from the profit before tax?
Accountant	We record what happens on the balance sheet. It's either a net deferred tax asset or liability.

5 **Later in the meeting the CEO asks more questions. Match them to the accountant's answers (a–g).**

1	Will this also be checked?	a	600 euros per hour.
2	Could you just go over it again?	b	I'm afraid that will be too late.
3	How is the profit calculated?	c	Every three months.
4	How much is your fee?	d	It's basically income minus expenses.
5	How often do they check?	e	Yes, of course. Let me try to explain it differently this time.
6	Who'll handle the presentation?		
7	How about if we send it in next week?	f	It should be. I'll ask Jürgen to make sure it's done.
		g	Susanne.

6   **Use the words from the box to complete the following conversation. Then explain – in your own words – what 'provision for income tax' and 'deferred income tax balances' mean.**

depends • so • clarify • mean • basically • exactly

Kathy	Hi Johannes. How's it going?
Johannes	It's not easy, all this English. We didn't do any of this on my course.
Kathy	Can I help?
Johannes	Well, maybe you could _____¹ a couple of things. Let's see. Ah, here we are. 'Provision for income taxes'. What does that _____²?
Kathy	OK. 'Provision' means putting money aside so that we have something to pay with later. So 'provision for income taxes' is talking about the current year's tax expense which will have to be paid in the future.
Johannes	Like provisional?
Kathy	Not _____³. 'Provisional' just means temporary, you know, not final. Like a provisional budget. It's not the final version.
Johannes	I see. And what about 'deferred income tax balances'. What does 'deferred' mean?
Kathy	_____⁴ put off to another day. The income has been recognized in the accounts, but the tax owing on that income will only be realized in the future.
Johannes	OK. How does that affect associated companies?
Kathy	Well, it _____⁵. Associated companies and affiliates are a special case. Deferred taxes are not normally recognized on undistributed earnings, but only if the plan is to re-invest the profits.
Johannes	_____⁶ if we don't invest the profits, we pay tax.
Kathy	Exactly.

7   **Now work with a partner to practise explaining and clarifying information. Each of you should explain a standard procedure from your workplace, and the other asks questions about it. Then swap partners and explain the procedure you have just heard to another person.**

In my office the procedure for claiming travel expenses is …

The way private people pay income tax in Germany is normally to …

USEFUL PHRASES

Clarifying information

Maybe you could clarify a couple of things.	– Sure./Certainly.
What do these figures mean again?	– Basically, they just mean that …
Can we just go over that one more time?	– Of course./No problem.
Could you repeat that, please?	– Sure, I said …
So, what you're saying is that the profits are too low.	– That's right./Exactly.
So, this column is wrong?	– Well, not exactly./it depends.
In other words, we'll need to send it by Friday?	– Exactly.
When did you say we'd be starting the audit?	– On …

8 Match these expressions with 'tax' to their definitions.

1	tax avoidance	a	someone who lives in another country for tax reasons
2	tax bracket	b	to introduce a new tax on something
3	tax evasion	c	to make the tax go up
4	tax exempt	d	when you don't have to pay tax on certain income
5	tax exile	e	to cancel a tax
6	to abolish tax	f	tells you what amount of tax to pay based on income
7	to impose tax	g	trying not to pay tax (legal)
8	to increase tax	h	trying not to pay tax (illegal)

9 Use words from the box to fill in the gaps.

> abolish • bracket • breaks • exempt • exile • increase • property • return

1 The government needs more money, so it is planning to _____ taxes.

2 He earns a lot of money – he must be in the highest tax _____ .

3 She lives there because she has to – she's a tax _____ .

4 They are planning to _____ the tax on large company cars, and replace it with a tax on all company cars.

5 She is a student, so she is tax _____ .

6 The government is planning to introduce new tax _____ for IT companies.

7 Don't buy a house this year – the _____ taxes are being abolished next March.

8 A tax _____ is the same as a tax declaration – it's a list of income and tax deductible expenditure for the tax authority.

10 An accountant from a Swiss parent company, Uta Meier, telephones the Internal Revenue Service (IRS) in the US to discuss the treatment of certain costs. What is the result of the discussion?

Uta These costs clearly relate to the repair and maintenance of our machines.

IRS But in your financial statements, you argue that this expenditure was to upgrade, and you have capitalized it all. At first glance, it appears clear that ...

Uta Excuse me, but you know as well as I do that the accounting and tax regulations allow for different definitions of what we can capitalize, and what we must expense

IRS Yes, but it's easy to work out the type of costs you have from the descriptions in your accounts. And based on our interpretation of the laws, this seems to be capital expenditure, which you can of course depreciate.

Uta We're going to take this further. I'm afraid I can't agree with your comments.

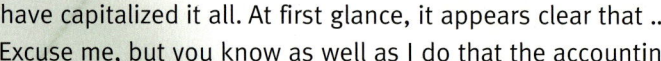

IRS   Look. I'm sorry but this conversation is going nowhere. I suggest you make a submission and send it to our office. We can then consider your arguments in detail.

Uta   Fine. I'll do it today. Thanks for your time.

IRS   You're welcome. Goodbye.

Uta   Bye.

| **VOCABULARY ASSISTANT** | to expense *als Kosten buchen*
submission *Antrag* |

11   **Find words from the conversation which mean the following:**

1   to improve a machine or equipment
2   written suggestion
3   an opinion of what something means

4   rules
5   to include as an asset
6   an explanation of what something means

USEFUL PHRASES

Polite language
Uta and the IRS agent didn't agree but they kept their conversation polite by using certain phrases and expressions to soften their statements. Most English speakers expect this type of 'polite' language and think people who don't use it are too direct and even impolite.
Here are some typical phrases you can use to 'soften' what you say.

Excuse me, but …
I'm sorry but …
I'm afraid that's not quite right.
We have a slight problem.

At first glance, it appears clear …
This seems to be …
Could you please …

12   **Use phrases from the box to 'soften' the following statements.**

1   *I can't agree with your comments. They don't make sense.*

3   *I disagree. You're wrong.*

4   *Your idea is rubbish.*

5   *Your calculations are full of mistakes.*

2   *This conversation is going nowhere. Call me back later.*

6   *You don't have the necessary experience to do this job.*

13   **The new head of your finance department wants to know about the taxation system in your country. He has also heard that the taxation system is closely connected with the financial reporting requirements. Write a report to him explaining the major points and referring to the relevant laws.**

14 Use the clues to complete the crossword.

Across:

1 suggestion, often in writing
5 a plan of how much you are going to spend
8 not permanent
11 the value of an item which has finished its useful life
12 opposite of loss
13 money you get for doing something

Down:

2 you might get this when someone dies
3 to take away; opposite of 'add'
4 wealth
6 excused from paying taxes: tax …
7 delayed
9 you pay this when you borrow money
10 putting money aside

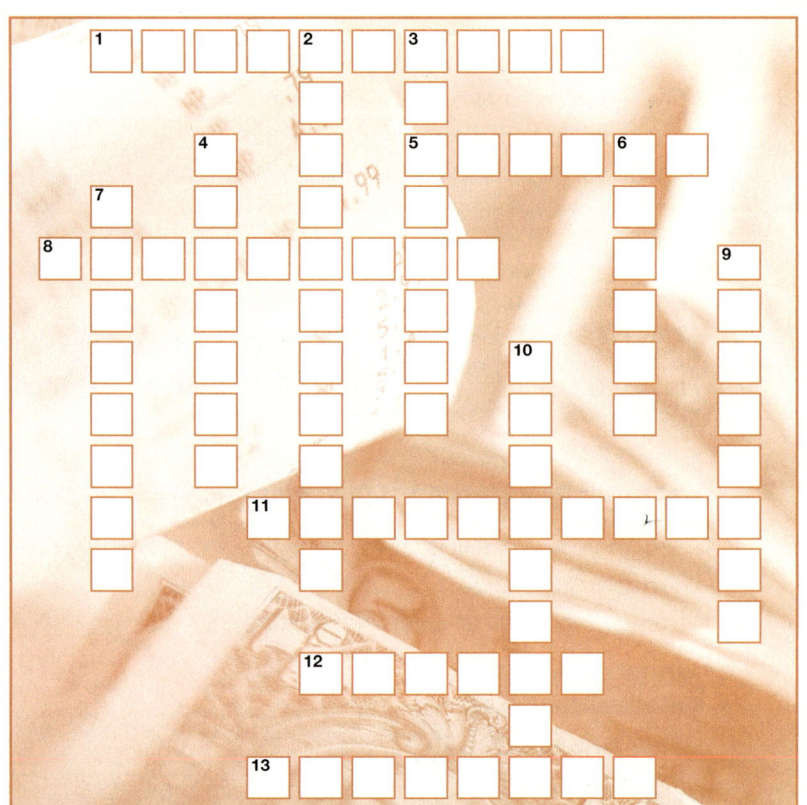

OPTIONAL READING

Taxation planning

The governments of some countries use the taxation system to promote investment. Taxation laws are enacted to encourage domestic and international

corporations to either invest or raise capital, and tax breaks are given to specific industries or to certain types of expenses to attract investors and consumers. As a result of these taxation measures, there is significant scope for taxation planning in some countries and companies would be well advised to use such opportunities to structure their business in the most tax effective manner.

For effective taxation planning, companies rely on tax specialists who must have an excellent understanding of both their clients' business and the various taxation laws. Companies turn to their tax advisers for help on all the taxes for which they are liable, such as income tax, sales tax, property tax and payroll tax. These tax specialists are normally Chartered Accountants and CPAs who are not only involved in the preparation of tax returns (compliance), but who also give advice on a multi-national company's domestic and foreign operations (consulting). Furthermore, they represent their clients before the tax authorities.

Over to you

Can you think of any tax breaks which the government in your country has introduced recently?
Where can a potential investor go for advice?
What tax advice would you give to an individual who comes to live and work in your country?

4 Auditing

START-UP **What does an auditor do? Decide whether the following statements are true or false and compare your results with a partner. Are there differences in the work of internal and external auditors?**

True = ☑   False = ☒

An auditor ...

1 spends time getting to know the business as well as the environment and the industry in which it operates. ☐

2 analyses the internal business and financial systems used to make and record transactions. ☐

3 gathers evidence on the financial control systems and the figures in the financial statements. ☐

4 gives advice on the business methods and transactions of the company. ☐

5 examines financial statements to determine whether they conform to generally accepted accounting principles. ☐

6 prepares the financial statements in accordance with the generally accepted accounting principles of the country where the enterprise operates. ☐

7 examines the management report and determines whether it conforms to the financial statements. ☐

8 guarantees the correctness of the figures presented in the accounts. ☐

9 provides consulting services. ☐

10 presents a written report to the management of the company, describing whether the accounting records, financial statements and management reports conform to legal requirements. ☐

11 maintains confidentiality and independence. ☐

DID YOU KNOW?

There are lots of different types of audits. The following types are often performed in government areas:
- **Performance auditing** is an independent evaluation of an organization's operations, intended to make it more efficient.
- **Financial audits** are similar to those performed in the public arena.
- **Compliance audits** determine whether the organization is following laws, regulations and contractual grant or loan agreements.
- **Investigative audits** are a result of allegations made against government employees or agencies relating to improper activities.

VOCABULARY ASSISTANT   allegations *Beschuldigungen*
improper *unzulässig*

1   Janet Hendley, a partner in an audit firm, calls Klaus Becker, the CFO of a German company. Read the dialogue, and then decide if the statements which follow are true or false.

Klaus   Becker.

Janet   Hi Klaus. It's Janet. You wanted to chat?

Klaus   Hi Janet. Great, you got my message. Thanks for getting back to me so quickly.

Janet   You're welcome. How can I help?

Klaus   Well, it's about your preliminary report. There are a couple of things I think we need to discuss.

Janet   Yeah sure. No problem. I have it in front of me.

Klaus   Hang on, I'll just find my notes. OK. The first point is on page 11. Third paragraph. What do you mean, exactly?

Janet   OK. Let's have a look. Oh yes. Capitalization of costs in your factories. We think that these costs should be expenses in the P&L.

Klaus   But ... no, sorry. I'm afraid I disagree. They were necessary for the upgrade of our plant. Surely you agree that we have to keep up with the competition?

Janet   Yes, of course. But lots of the items we tested are clearly normal repair and maintenance expenses. You can't really justify including such costs under machine upgrades.

Klaus   I see it differently. Our machines have been developed to produce a wider variety of products, to improve the running efficiency of the equipment, to keep us in business. This was a sizeable investment on our part. The figure we're talking about shows the commitment we've made to the future. I mean, we're going to be getting benefits from these upgrades for years. Our balance sheet should show this.

Janet   I'm sorry. These figures are too material for us to ignore. There are some expenses which ...

Klaus   Companies do this all the time, and I might add, their auditors accept it. I suggest you consider this again. I'm sure you'll find it's reasonable when you think about how important these investments were to this company.

Janet   All right. We'll look at these costs again. Let's move on the next point.

VOCABULARY ASSISTANT	efficiency *Leistungsfähigkeit* to justify *rechtfertigen* material *wesentlich*

True or false?

1   Janet wants to talk to Klaus about a report.   ❑

2   Janet thinks that capitalization of costs should be expenses in the P&L.   ❑

3   Klaus agrees with Janet on this point.   ❑

4   Klaus thinks capitalization of costs should be classed under machine upgrades.   ❑

5   Klaus's reasoning is that the upgrades are really investments in the future.   ❑

6   Janet agrees to reconsider his opinion.   ❑

2 **Find the sentence on the right which is closest in meaning to the sentence on the left.**

1   We have to keep up with the competition.

   a   We can ignore the competition.
   b   We can't ignore the competition.

2   You can't really justify spending so much money on office equipment.

   a   You can't defend your actions.
   b   You can defend your actions.

3   This plan is designed to keep us in business.

   a   This is a plan to start a business.
   b   This is a plan to get business.

4   This was a sizeable investment on our part.

   a   We spent very little money on this.
   b   We spent a lot of money on this.

5   These figures are too material for us to ignore.

   a   The figures are very high.
   b   The figures are very low.

6   I suggest you consider this again.

   a   Have another think about it.
   b   Forget it.

7   I'm sure you'll find it's reasonable.

   a   You think this is fair.
   b   I think this is fair.

3 **Here is the follow-up conversation between Klaus and Janet, but the sentences are in the wrong order. Re-arrange them so that the conversation makes sense.**

	Janet	Glad to be of assistance.
	Janet	Good to hear.
	Janet	Tuesday? No, sorry, I'm afraid I'm busy on Tuesday. What about Wednesday morning? At, say, 9 am?
1	*Janet*	Hendley and Sanderson. Janet Hendley speaking.
	Janet	Hi Klaus. How's it going?
	Janet	Yes, you too. Bye.
	Janet	Yes, yes. Actually, we had a meeting this morning. I was just about to send you an email. You'll be glad to hear that the partners have agreed with your proposal.

	Klaus	Yes, that sounds good, Wednesday at 9. So, Janet, I'll see you then. Have a good weekend.
	Klaus	Bye.
	Klaus	Erm. One other thing. There are some other things I'd like to go over with you, but I'd prefer to do it in person, not over the phone. Could you come by the office next week sometime? Tuesday, say?
2	*Klaus*	Hi Janet. It's Klaus.
	Klaus	Listen, Janet. I'm just calling to find out if you've had a chance to look at those capitalization of costs yet. You know – our machine upgrades?
	Klaus	Not too bad. Our latest sales figures are quite good so the boss is happy.
	Klaus	That's great. It'll really help.

4 Work with a partner to practise making a telephone call. Use phrases from the box below.

PARTNER FILE → Partner A page 50
Partner B page 52

USEFUL PHRASES

Telephone phrases
Hello, this is … from … .
May I speak to …, please?
Could you put me through to … ?
– Janet speaking.
Hello, Janet. It's Klaus.

Making appointments
Could you come by the office next week?
How/What about Monday at 9.30?
Can you make Tuesday afternoon?
– No, I'm sorry. I'm busy then.
– Yes, that sounds good.

5 Two colleagues from an auditing firm are discussing the latest financial scandal. Whose opinion do you agree with most?

Heidi	Have you seen the latest?
Philip	What's that? About Hamrenicoh PLC?
Heidi	Yeah. And it's not the only one. Every week there's a new scandal. It's going to change how we do our job.
Philip	How? Our role is only to give an opinion based on estimates. We can't review every little thing in detail.
Heidi	Oh, come on. Investors expect financial information to be correct. And I think it's fair enough. If they find out that, I don't know, that assets have been overstated by 50%, then they're going to be annoyed. I would be too.
Philip	*We* don't overstate anything.
Heidi	But we're expected to find these things. That's what we're paid to do.

Philip Hang on a minute. Our job is to review the information provided to us by the management of a company. We have to assume that they're being honest. We're not police officers.
Heidi But …
Philip Let me finish. Look, there are legal mechanisms to deal with people who commit fraud. The auditing profession has it's own regulations and investors trust this. It's tried and tested.
Heidi All I'm saying is that investors have a right to rely on the financial information they read, and we're paid to check exactly that. Self-regulation may not be enough. And the trend is …
Philip I agree that it's a bit strange that we're paid by the same people who we audit, but it's always been this way and I don't see how that can be changed, do you?

Discuss the issue of auditor-client relationship with your class. What responsibilities do auditors have in their relationship with their clients? How is this relationship regulated in your country or other countries that you know? Is it enough?

6 **Auditors often have to write or present reports on the financial information they have audited. This is especially important for enterprises with branches or subsidiaries in foreign countries. Look at the following sentences and decide which graph or chart goes best with the description.**

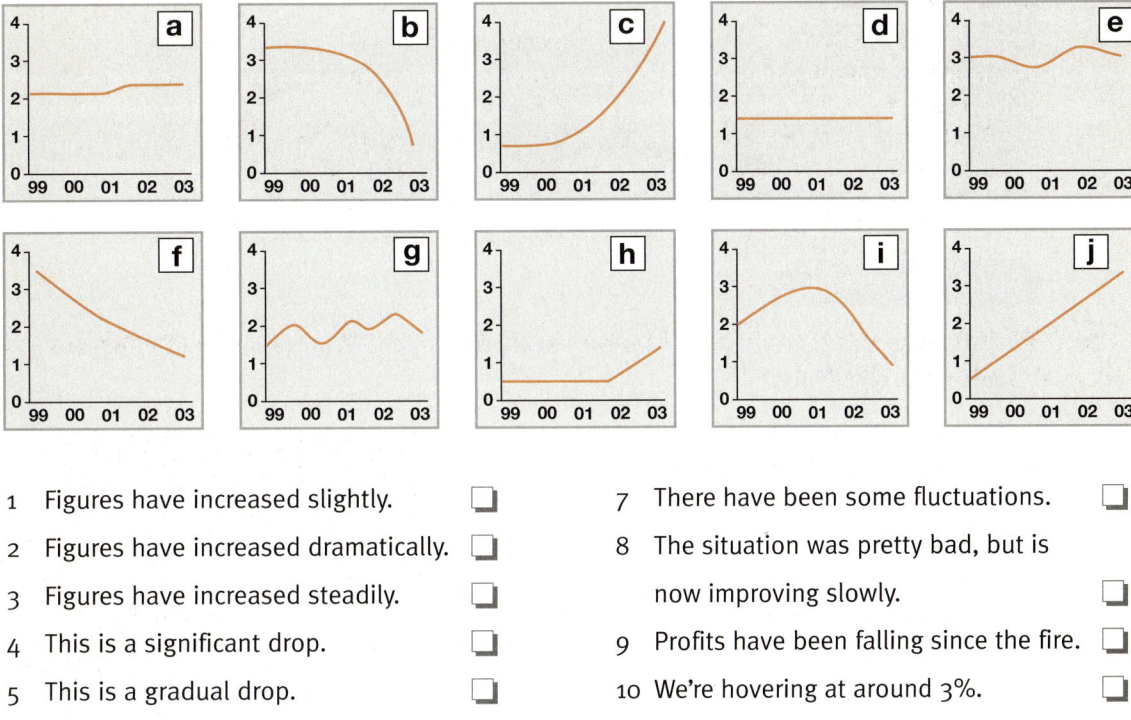

1	Figures have increased slightly.	☐
2	Figures have increased dramatically.	☐
3	Figures have increased steadily.	☐
4	This is a significant drop.	☐
5	This is a gradual drop.	☐
6	The situation is stable.	☐

7	There have been some fluctuations.	☐
8	The situation was pretty bad, but is now improving slowly.	☐
9	Profits have been falling since the fire.	☐
10	We're hovering at around 3%.	☐

7 **Now choose the option which makes most sense.**

"Have a look at this. Last year was really good. Profits *fell / rose* [1] dramatically after we launched Glenogen. And here you can see how it affected the rest of the market. CFL remained *stable / gradual* [2], which was a bit of a surprise, but Junfil was hit quite badly – sales *increased / decreased* [3] to almost non-existent. Now look here. This next graph shows what we think will happen next year. Good news again. Everything's going *up / down* [4]."

8 **Work with a partner to practise describing graphs or trends. Use phrases from exercise 6.**

PARTNER FILE   Partner A   page 51
                Partner B   page 53

9 **Now write a report on some figures from your company or from one of your clients. Explain the movement from one year to the next, giving the cause and the result. Here are some phrases which might help.**

USEFUL PHRASES

Explaining causes and results

Cause	**Result**
This happened because …	It could lead to …
This (increase/decrease) is due to …	What could happen is …
This is a result of …	Because of this, we'll see …

OPTIONAL READING

Read this example of an extract from an independent auditors' report in the USA and answer the questions.

To Share Owners and Board of Directors of Megatrap Corp

We have audited the accompanying statement of financial position of Megatrap Corp and consolidated affiliates as of December 31, 2003 and 2002, and the statements of earnings, changes in share owners' equity and cash flows for each of the years in the three-year period ended December 31, 2003. These consolidated financial statements are the responsibility of the Company's management. We have to express an opinion on these consolidated financial statements based on our audits.

We conducted our audits in accordance with auditing standards generally accepted in the United States of America. Under these standards we have to plan and perform the audit to obtain reasonable assurance that the financial statements do not have any material misstatement. We examined on a test basis the evidence supporting the figures and disclosures in the financial statements. We also assessed the accounting principles used and significant estimates made by management, and we evaluated the presentation of the statements.

In our opinion, the aforementioned financial statements present fairly, in all material respects, the financial position of Megatrap Corp and consolidated affiliates at December 31, 2003 and 2002, and the results of their operations and their cash flows for each of the years in the three-year period ended December 31, 2003, in conformity with accounting principles generally accepted in the United States of America.

Over to you

According to the report, an audit does several things. What is mentioned?

What documents did the auditors look at?

In what ways is this report different to those used in your country?

Management accounting

Cost accounting is about manufacturing and sales costs. But what exactly is management accounting? Which of the following are true statements?

1 Management accountants prepare information which managers use to make decisions.

2 Management accountants sometimes suggest ways to improve financial performance.

3 Management accountants may also analyse non-financial data.

4 Management accounts are normally for internal use only.

1 A new commercial manager, who has been sent in from the overseas parent company, is having a meeting with the German CFO.

Manager I'm sorry, but the external accounts don't help me much. Doesn't matter if they're in English or German. I need information from you which will help me run this department.

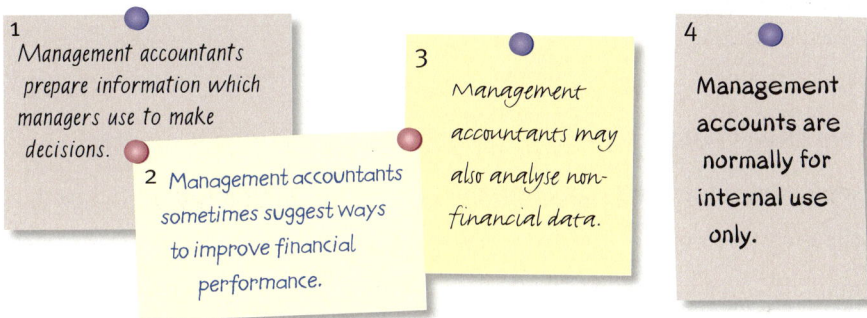

CFO What exactly would you like?

Manager Well, for example, I need something which tells me about the profit we make on our customers, with some sort of break-down based on the size of the company. I want to compare the money we make to the size of the customer.

CFO Sure. We can do that. And how about the costs per customer?

Manager Exactly. How much we spend on each customer, compared to the size of their orders.

CFO That should be possible.

Manager Great. Also, the profit made per employee. I would like to know where we are profitable and which employees we make our money.

CFO You realize that this is going to be a lot of work for my department.

Manager Yes. I know. But it's very important for me. Can I also have a complete breakdown of our overhead expenses, and the allocation of them to each of the products that we sell?

CFO OK. How would you like all this information to be presented?

Manager In plain English, please. So that even I can understand it.

Make a list of what the CFO needs to supply. How do you think he should present this information? What kind of reports or documents would be most effective?

2 **Find words in the dialogue above to complete the table.**

VERB	NOUN	ADJECTIVE
to allocate	_____ 1	—
to complete	completion	_____ 2
to cost	_____ 3	costly
to employ	_____ 4/employer	employable
to inform	_____ 5	informative
to produce	_____ 6	productive
to profit	profit	_____ 7
to sell	_____ 8	—

Now use the correct form of words from the table to complete the sentences.

a   We have far too much work – we need to _____ an assistant to help us.

b   Everything we do depends on having accurate _____ .

c   The company _____ electrical goods like photocopiers and scanners.

d   We can't have new laptops for everyone because it's simply too _____.

e   The pre-tax _____ was over € 12 bn.

f   We've been _____ the conference room on the ground floor. Let's meet down there at 2 pm.

g   They hope to _____ the report by Friday.

h   We always have the highest _____ at Christmas.

3 **Look at the Statement of Cash Flows on the next page. Are the following statements true or false?**

1   Amortization of goodwill and other intangibles rose in 2002.
2   More dividends were paid in 2002 than in 2001.
3   Net earnings increased from 2000 to 2002.
4   Depreciation and amortization of property, plant and equipment went up in 2002.
5   Inventories remained stable during the period 2000–2002.
6   There were no additions to property, plant and equipment in 2002.
7   Deferred income taxes fell in 2002.
8   Cash for operating activities was more than cash for investing activities.

DID YOU KNOW?

The regulatory authorities of various countries have made it mandatory for certain enterprises (eg, publicly listed companies) to produce and present a report on the movement of cash in any given year. This statement is called the 'Source and Application of Funds', the 'Statement of Cash Flows' or the 'Cash Flow Statement'.

Statement of Cash Flows

For the years ended December 31 (In millions)	2002	2001	2000
Cash flows – operating activities			
Net earnings	$ 9,734	$ 8,919	$ 8,910
Adjustments to reconcile net earnings to cash provided from operating activities			
Cumulative effect of accounting changes	0	212	0
Depreciation and amortization of property, plant and equipment	3,574	3,475	3,118
Amortization of goodwill and other intangibles	1,837	1,987	1,887
Earnings (before accounting changes) retained	0	0	0
Deferred income taxes	965	756	545
Decrease (increase) in current receivables	1,274	1,177	1,571
Decrease (increase) in inventories	(617)	(847)	189
Decrease (increase) in accounts payable	2,647	3,197	2,948
Decrease (increase) in insurance liabilities and reserves	4,490	5,612	6,765
Provision for losses on financing receivables	1,964	1,299	1,578
All other operating activities	4,966	689	32
Cash from operating activities	30,834	26,476	27,543
Cash flows – investing activities			
Additions to property, plant and equipment	(16,222)	(12,388)	(13,094)
Dispositions of property, plant and equipment	5,609	4,512	5,436
Net increase in financing receivables	(10,755)	(8,287)	(7,339)
Payments for principal businesses purchased	(8,618)	(1,276)	(6,376)
All other investing activities	(1,388)	(4,858)	(4,286)
Cash used for investing activities	(31,374)	(22,297)	(25,659)
Cash flows – financing activities			
Net increase (decrease) in borrowings (maturities of 90 days or more)	18,594	(3,590)	1,844
Newly issued debt (maturities longer than 90 days)	18,866	36,644	30,866
Repayments and other reductions (maturities longer than 90 days)	(40,056)	(32,918)	(30,667)
Net dispositions (purchases)	1,732	1,288	(1,466)
Dividends paid	(3,655)	(3,455)	(3,298)
All other financing activities	266	655	(7)
Cash from (used for) financing activities	(4,253)	(1,376)	(2,728)
Increase (decrease) in cash and equivalents during year	(4,793)	2,803	(844)
Cash and equivalents at beginning of year	18,278	15,475	16,319
Cash and equivalents at end of year	$ 13,485	$ 18,278	$ 15,475
Supplemental disclosure of cash flows information			
Cash paid during the year for interest	(9,475)	(10,366)	(8,838)
Cash recovered (paid) during the year for income taxes	(1,288)	(1,909)	(1,678)

VOCABULARY ASSISTANT

dispositions *Veräußerung* maturity *Fälligkeit* to reconcile *ausgleichen* supplemental disclosure *ergänzende Angaben*

4   **Match these words from the Statement of Cash Flows with their meanings.**

1	dividend	a	money that is owed
2	cash	b	purchase price minus real value of assets
3	plant	c	reduction in value due to wear and tear
4	amortization	d	money paid out to shareholders
5	goodwill	e	writing an intangible asset off over a number of years
6	cumulative	f	increasing by successive additions
7	depreciation	g	coins, bank notes, or something that can be easily exchanged for these
8	debt	h	building and equipment for manufacturing

5   **Work with a partner. Look at the Statement of Cash Flows again. One of you explain in your own words where the money has come from. The other explain where it has gone. Together write a brief report for your manager.**

6   **Here are some expressions with 'cash'. Match the sentences with the pictures.**

1   I'm totally out of cash.
2   We would expect cash in advance so that we can buy the materials.
3   Cash on delivery, please.
4   The A120 is the best – it's a real cash cow.
5   Use the petty cash to pay for the tea, and we'll sort it out later.
6   They're trying to raise cash by selling some assets, but they've only got until the end of the month. It's going to be tight.

7   **In the following meeting, the directors of a company are discussing the future direction of the company and the budgeting process. As you read, match the people with their job titles.**

R&D Director

Managing Director

Marketing Director

Investment Director

Finance Director

Secretary

Beate   So we've agreed that Sally's team will produce those figures by the end of the month. Got that, Per? Good. OK, I'd like to move to the next item on the agenda, which is the budget for the upcoming year. Peter, would you please give a short overview of your research into the market, and your conclusions?

Peter   Sure. As you all know, my department has been extensively researching the market and the economic conditions we'll be facing in the short term. It's quite clear that events of recent years have unsettled the market greatly. Both investors and consumers are convinced that it won't get better, probably for a long time. Investors are looking for solid companies, and consumers don't just throw their cash around like they used to. We think that the situation will remain like it is in the middle term. This is a time for consolidation, not expansion.

Beate   Simon, what does R&D think about this?

Simon   It's a pretty negative outlook. We've been working really hard to come up with some great ideas, and maybe now's the time to launch some of our new products.

Gavin   And our investment programme has been ready to go for months. We can't just wait and hope that things get better. Our strategy has always been to lead the market, not sit back and cruise along.

Beate   Peter?

Peter   Ideas and investments don't mean cash in the bank. Consumers simply don't have the confidence to spend their money on fancy new products. And as for expansion, I think the good old days are long gone. We should be cutting back.

Beate   Sally, how do you feel about all this?

Sally   We're talking about budgets for the upcoming year. Everybody's forecasts seem to indicate hard times ahead. And we don't even have the money to spend. How are we going to service more debt, or raise more cash in the capital markets?

Beate   So despite our great ideas and investment plans, it seems the reality is that our budgets for this year will have to be tight.

8 Use words from each box to make useful word partnerships. Then match them to the definitions below.

negative • hard • economic • next • middle • cut • capital • investment

back • outlook • item • term • plan • times • conditions • markets

1 what will be discussed after this
2 the state of the economy
3 a programme for getting money to grow
4 a bad view of the future
5 a reduction in something
6 difficult situation
7 a period between soon and the distant future
8 a place where you can buy and sell debt or equity securities

9 Here are some useful phrases for meetings. Write the number in the correct box. Can you add any more phrases from the conversation in exercise 7?

1 We have to make a decision today about ...
2 So, in other words ...
3 Anything to add, Harry?
4 What I want to look at is ...
5 Can you say that again?
6 You *did* say the 24th, didn't you?
7 Let me just go over what we have agreed.
8 What I'm saying is ...
9 Shall we move on to the next item?
10 To sum up then, ...
11 I'd like to move on if I may.
12 Perhaps we could discuss that at lunch?
13 Our aim today is to ...
14 I didn't quite catch that.
15 Sally?

stating objectives
1

asking for contributions

moving on

dealing with communication problems
2

summarizing

10 Now try to use phrases from above in a meeting role-play. Work with a partner to discuss next year's budget. One of you should act as chairperson.

PARTNER FILE

Partner A page 51
Partner B page 53

11 **Bring a real budget to class. If it is in German, you will need to explain the key words. Then present it to the class, and be prepared to answer their questions.**

The future of accounting

The traditional view of accountants as merely 'bean counters' is slowly becoming a thing of the past. For centuries, accountants have been employed to report on the numbers. They have sat there in their little corner, surrounded by stacks of paper and computer printouts, and have told us whether or not we have made a profit. But more and more, accountants are finding that management doesn't need them to report on the numbers. With today's technology, management already has access to software programs which do this work for them.

So what will the future accountant do? According to Mr Hamilton-Smythe, the Managing Director of KHZ Enterprises, the large international manufacturing company, accountants will be employed "to help companies *change* the numbers. Their expertise, and knowledge of the business will be called upon to prepare strategies. They will become consultants and advisers. And their skills will need to change accordingly. They will be involved in international meetings, in giving presentations, running international teams, writing reports and making decisions."

This is going to require a significant change in the general public's opinion of accountants, who in turn will need to develop skills not traditionally associated with the job. The image of the guy in the corner with the stacks of paper will change to one of a high flyer, someone who is critical to the success of the organization.

Over to you

What do you think the future of accounting looks like?
What skills will you need to be successful in this profession?
How will you prepare yourself for the future?

6 Investment

A US manager is thinking of investing in a German 'Mittelstand' company and you are advising her. She has a list of questions for the German owner. Can you think of any more she should ask?

What is the proportion of debt to equity in the business?

Who are the major clients?

At what rate have they depreciated the plant?

1 The management of a US company is discussing the possibility of investing in a German enterprise. List the factors they mention. How does this list compare with your questions from the Start-up?

Anne	So, can we agree at least that it will be most cost effective to invest in an existing business? That way, we will be able to utilize the local knowledge of the personnel currently running the business.
Luis	Yeah, I think so. The question is how exactly. Do we buy the company or only the assets? There's a lot to think about. For instance, the due diligence process, although that won't affect the mechanics of our acquisition. What will we have to consider, Allen? You're the international lawyer.

Ziel GmbH

Purchase Price	1,900
Net Assets	(1,350)
Goodwill	550
Ordinary Share Capital	1,100
Reserves	250
Equity	1,350

Allen	Lots of things, takeover rules, European Union regulations on competition and the accounting legislation. Dana, can you tell us something about that?
Dana	Actually, the accounting regulations in Germany aren't such a big issue. More important will be the effect of our acquisition on our balance sheet. The goodwill component is huge and we have to be aware of the impact this is going to have.
Tom	What do you mean?
Dana	Well, the amortization of goodwill may lead to large expenses in the coming years. Our profit may be seriously affected. We could perhaps only impair the goodwill, which means to write it down only when its fair value has decreased. That'll be an interesting discussion with the auditors.

2   **Use words from the conversation to complete the table. The first one is done for you.**

VERB	NOUN	VERB	NOUN
to acquire	_____ a	to _____ e	investment
to _____ b	agreement	to legislate	_____ f
to _____ c	consideration	to _____ g	thought
to discuss	_____ d	to _____ h	utilization

Now use the correct form of the words above to complete the email below.

Hi guys

I've been looking at the figures for the Berlin project. I _____ [1] we need to find ways
to make the _____ [2] more profitable. One idea may be to _____ [3] the
plant in Mitte, but this will need _____ [4] from the local authorities. We could also
_____ [5] in the Marzahn plant, but this may cause problems with the local monopoly
_____ [6]. Maybe we could _____ [7] it at Friday's meeting. Any _____ [8]?

Sam

3   **Here is another email. This time the CFO of a British company is writing to the head of the German subsidiary. What is Hermann's job?**

Hello Dieter

Thanks for your email. As you know, before we can agree to your investing in the new plant in Italy,
we need to have a clear description of the project. I've listed the main points below. If you have any
questions give me a call, but remember I'm away the first two weeks of December. I've copied this
email to Hermann as I'm sure he will be responsible for producing much of the information.

1   audited financial statements of the plant's current owners
2   planned sources of supply
3   possible suppliers of capital goods and services
4   anticipated output
5   markets and distribution channels
6   competition
7   a summary of project costs

Best wishes
KJ

1 selected

VOCABULARY ASSISTANT   anticipated *erwartet*
distribution channel *Vertriebsweg*

Read the email again and then decide if the following statements are true or false.

		true	false
1	Hermann is senior to Dieter in the company hierarchy.	❏	❏
2	The British company has already decided to invest in the new plant.	❏	❏
3	KJ wants Dieter to describe the project in more detail.	❏	❏
4	KJ wants financial information about how the plant has performed in the past.	❏	❏
5	KJ wants to know about other similar plants in the market.	❏	❏
6	KJ is very interested in how many people work in the plant.	❏	❏
7	KJ needs to have the completed report by 7 December.	❏	❏

4   **The CFO of a European corporation is talking about differences in accounting practices in other countries. Match each comment with a point from his list.**

- **taxation system**
- **goodwill**
- **leased products**
- **inventory**
- **financial instruments**
- **income statements**

If we are thinking about raising capital in overseas markets the reporting requirements of those markets are obviously important. I've summarized some of the major points on this slide – let's go through them briefly.

1 *It may be possible to measure all of these at their fair value, which would allow the recognition of unrealized gains.*

2 *This may have been developed completely separately from the accounting systems, and may provide considerable opportunities for taxation planning.*

3 *Typical of these is the Profit and Loss Account.*

4 *This can be acquired or self-generated – of course it may have to be recognized as an asset, if certain criteria are met.*

5 *Here we're talking about things which we don't actually own – they go back to their owners after a certain amount of time. They require different disclosure in the Balance Sheet, and the GAAP of different countries can require different classification, normally finance or operating.*

6 *The methods used to measure this can vary considerably. The normal ones are FIFO, which means 'first in first out', LIFO or 'last in first out', or average cost, which is somewhere between the two. All give a different value for what we hold.*

5 **Do you know of any cross border investments that have failed? Discuss with a partner, and try to analyse possible reasons for the failure.**

6 **Read the following extracts from a speech. What do you think Kathrin Schneider does for a living?**

Good morning, ladies and gentlemen. My name is Kathrin Schneider. I'd like to thank you first of all for giving me the opportunity to come here today and talk to you about the intercultural issues facing enterprises with cross-border interests. Although I am not an accountant I hope to give you some information which will help you in your dealings abroad. If you don't mind, I would prefer to answer any questions you may have at the end.

There'll be three parts to my presentation. I'll start with a short description of the general issues faced by managers today. Then we'll look at some of the issues in more detail using some of the data I have collected. Finally we'll look at how you can approach these problems and create successful international teams. There will be a comprehensive hand-out at the end, so there's no need to take notes unless you really want to.

(later)

So, what can we conclude from all this? We all know that globalization has been a buzzword for many years now. All of us have been involved in or seen companies expand across borders and we have seen some mergers collapse. I think that my research has shown that one of the main reasons for such collapses is that management has ignored the intercultural factors facing the members of teams working in an intercultural environment. I hope my presentation has made you aware of some of the factors which affect the ability of people from different cultures to work together.

I will now be happy to take any questions from the floor, and perhaps even discuss some of these issues further. Yes, the gentleman on the right?

Now answer the questions.

1 Look back at the opening paragraph. What do you think the title of the talk is?
2 In the second paragraph Kathrin Schneider says that she has divided her talk into three main topics. What are they?
3 Now look again at the final part of the talk. What do you think the main point of the talk was?

7 **Here are some useful phrases for giving a presentation. Match the parts so that they make sense.**

1	If you don't mind, I would prefer to		happy to take		really want to.
2	I will now be		some of the issues in		you can create successful international teams.
3	There'll be		take notes unless you		at the end.
4	I'll start with		answer any questions you may have		my presentation.
5	Then we'll look at		look at how		any questions.
6	Finally we'll		a short description of		the general issues.
7	There's no need to		three parts to		more detail.

8 **Now prepare a short presentation on a project you are working on at the moment, or perhaps a procedure you are very familiar with. You may like to use the following structure to plan your talk:**

> **DID YOU KNOW?**
>
> **Planning a talk**
> No matter what language it is in, a good talk has a very clear structure.
>
> **Introduction**
> Explain who you are, and how your talk will benefit the audience.
> Give a brief outline of what you plan to say.
>
> **Main body**
> Go into detail about your different topics.
>
> **Summary**
> Briefly remind your audience what you have covered, and repeat your main points.
>
> **Conclusion**
> Stress your main message, and make sure the audience knows how they can use this message.

9 **Complete the puzzle to find the hidden word.**

1 the difference between the amount actually paid for a company and its book value
2 the ways that goods are delivered to the customer: distribution …
3 taking control of a company by buying most of its shares: a …
4 another word for 'abroad'
5 a company, piece of land, etc bought by a company: an …
6 a company's raw material and finished or unfinished products that haven't been sold yet

10 **Work with a partner. Use the role cards in the partner file to have a meeting about investing abroad.**

PARTNER FILE ➔ Partner A page 51
Partner B page 53

OPTIONAL READING

Read these statements about globalization and the role of accountants.
Which opinions (if any) do you agree with?

 Accountants are responsible for reporting on the future profitability of an international merger or takeover. It is the accountants who produce financial information so they are best equipped to analyse the numbers of a potential partner or target. The accountants should see the opportunities for growth.

 Accountants are only responsible for checking the figures provided by the company or organization. They have no skill in seeing opportunities for companies to expand.

Accountants have no people skills. They are not trained in the finer art of communication. They should there-fore be left in their  offices to punch the numbers. They can't be let loose with representatives from the potential partner!

 Accountants nowadays have ever-increasing responsibilities. They are on the boards of directors of companies all over the world. They are involved in negotiations and meetings every day. They are no longer machines dressed up in suits. They have had to improve their communication and interpersonal skills.

 Accounting rules are basically the same all over. Maybe we'll have to learn a few more things, but our job will be basically the same.

 Accounting regulations are different in every country. Globalization will lead to accountants having to be up to date on the latest developments, and not only those of the country they work in.

Over to you

How do you think globalization has affected – or will affect – you?
What about the next generation of accountants? How do you think their jobs will be different?

Test yourself!

See how much accounting vocabulary you've learned.
Use the clues to complete the crossword puzzle.

Across

3 the process to reduce the value of an intangible asset to zero, over a specified number of years

5 describes how the capital value of an asset goes down over time

7 happening before something else: a ... report or a ... meeting

9 another word for land or buildings

11 the list of people employed and paid by a company

13 the person who examines the business and financial records of a company or organization

15 debts of a business

19 the money that a company or organization receives from its business

20 the latest version of an item which, due to new technology or processes, replaces the older version

22 statement of the financial position of a company at a specific time: ... sheet

23 cannot be seen or touched; often used with the word 'assets'

26 the amount of money that a company is owed

Down

1 the process of including the figures of subsidiaries and affiliates in the accounts of a holding company

2 American English word for 'stock on hand'

4 the expenses of a company which can't be charged to a particular product, department, etc: ... expenses

6 a person who lives outside the country for tax reasons (two words)

8 profits paid to shareholders of a company

10 adapting a company's figures to give the best possible picture: ... accounting

12 another word for the purchase of something, such as another company or a piece of land

14 a piece of business that is done between two parties, such as buying or selling

16 a person or company that is owed money

17 the money you pay when you buy something: ... price

18 a company which is owned by another (parent) company

21 the money spent to buy another company, which is more than the fair value of the tangible assets

24 a written contract to rent a piece of equipment or a building for a period of time

25 things of value which belong to a company or person

Partner file

Unit 1

You work in the finance department of your company. Today a new colleague from your overseas parent company is coming to the office for the first time. (He or she doesn't speak German.) You have been asked to welcome the new colleague, show him/her around the office and make him/her feel comfortable. At the end you should introduce your new colleague to the head of the department.

Unit 2

You're in trouble. You've just spilt coffee all over this document, and you need it for an important meeting in a few minutes. Phone your colleague (Partner B) and ask him/her to give you the missing numbers.

Christmas party budget
(last year's figures in brackets)

Transport	€7000	(€6
Food	€6000	(€
Drink	€	(€19,564.57)
Band (3 hours)	€5000	(€4566.00)
Breakages	€0	(€ 6.00)
Insurance (1.5 m liability)	€200	(€0)
Total	€38,200	(€

Unit 4, Exercise 4

You would like to arrange a meeting with a colleague to discuss your ideas for some new software for the department. It is very urgent as you have a meeting next Friday with the head of your department and your boss expects results. Phone your colleague and find a suitable time to meet. (You will need your diary.)

Unit 4, Exercise 8

Look at the following graphs. They are incomplete. You have one part, while your partner has the missing part. Work with your partner to complete the information.

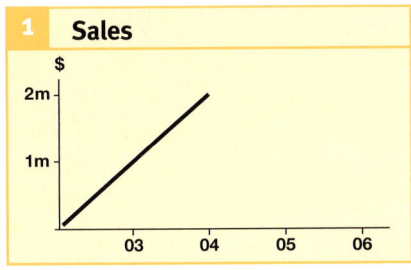

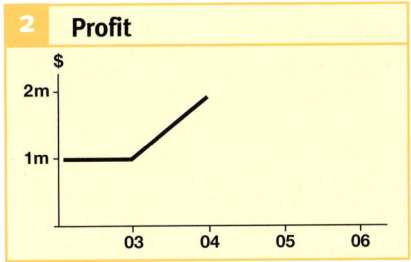

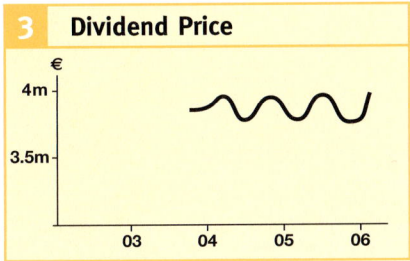

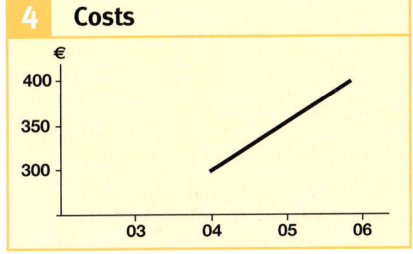

Unit 5

Times are tough. Costs have to be reduced. But where? As the MD (Managing Director) of a large international conglomerate, you have to reduce your budget for next year. Make some notes on how the finance department can save costs (eg, less staff, more software), and be prepared to explain your position in a preliminary meeting with your Chief Financial Officer.

Unit 6

You work in the finance department of a large US based conglomerate, and are currently at a trade fair in Leipzig. Your boss has asked you to look out for European companies interested in working with you – your company needs to get a foothold in the expanding European market. You are about to meet up with someone from a medium-sized European company which is looking for investment from abroad. This could be your chance. Your aim in the meeting is to decide what information you need from the other company, and what happens next.

Partner B	**Partner file**

Unit 1

It is your first day in your new job as a member of the finance department in one of your company's German subsidiaries. You do not speak German, but hope to start taking lessons soon. One of your new colleagues will meet you and show you around the company. Make small talk and ask questions about the company. (How many people work there? Do they have a canteen? Does the company offer language classes? etc)

Unit 2

The following document has just been faxed to you, but some of the information has not printed properly. Unfortunately you need all the information in order to brief your boss. You are just wondering what to do when your phone rings.

Christmas party budget
(last year's figures in brackets)

Transport	€7,000	(€6,543.23)
Food	€6,000	(€5,647.98)
Drink	€20,000	(€ ...)
Band (3 hours)	€6,000	(€ ...)
Breakages	€0	(€45,456.00)
Insurance (... liability)	€200	(€ ...)
Total	€...	(€81,777.78)

Unit 4, Exercise 4

You are looking through your diary for next week when the phone rings. You see from the number on your display that it is a colleague. Answer it. (You are very busy next week and it will be difficult to schedule any new appointments but you might be able to fit something in if it is important!)

Unit 4, Exercise 8

Look at the following graphs. They are incomplete. You have one part, while your partner has the missing part. Work with your partner to complete the information.

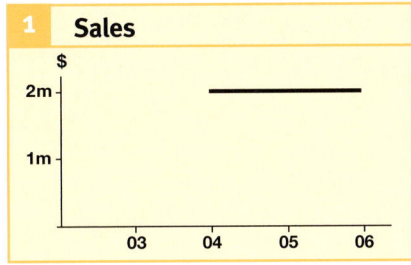

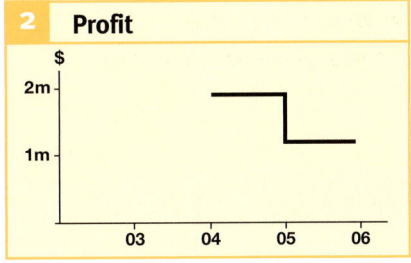

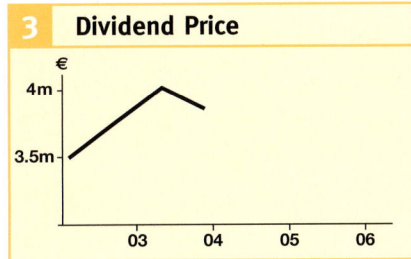

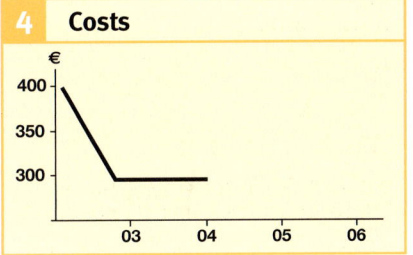

Unit 5

Times are tough. Costs have to be reduced. But where? As the CFO (Chief Financial Officer) of a large international conglomerate, you have to defend your budget for next year. Make some notes on why the employees in your department are so important, and be prepared to defend your position in a preliminary meeting with your boss, the Managing Director.

Unit 6

You are at a trade fair in Leipzig, representing a medium-sized European company which is looking for investment from abroad. You meet up with a representative from a large US-based conglomerate who sounds interested. Your aim in the meeting is to decide what information you need from the other company, and what happens next.

Answer key

Unit 1

Start-up *Possible answers:*
internal auditor
external auditor
public accountant
management accountant
bookkeeper
tax adviser
business consultant
financial controller

2 1 Mr Senkel will be with you in a moment.
2 Did you have a nice flight?
3 Would you like some coffee?
4 Sorry to keep you waiting.
5 Please come in and take a seat.
6 He's just finishing a phone call.
7 It's nice to meet you.

3 1 absolutely   5 very
2 start   6 bad
3 know   7 fairly
4 fill

4 *Possible answers:*
Safe topics: sport, weather, travel
Unsafe topics: religion, politics

7 1 publicly-traded company
2 English-speaking countries
3 accepted practice
4 local accounting standards
5 outside parties

8 1 the matching principle
2 the going concern principle
3 the prudence principle
4 the consistency principle

9 NB: The background and historical setting of accounting in different countries can lead to different ways of applying these rules. The prudence concept, for example, might therefore be stricter in one country than another.

10 1 False   5 False
2 True   6 False
3 True   7 False
4 True

11 It seems that Charles and Sabine both know that creative accounting exists. Maybe they have different opinions about how dangerous it is and what the consequences might be if they push the principles too far. But they both know that there are possibilities to structure their business in a way to take advantage of the existing principles.

12 1 e   2 f   3 g   4 b
5 a   6 c   7 d

13 1 debts   5 liability
2 liabilities   6 liabilities
3 debt   7 debt
4 liabilities

14 1 ✓   2 ✓   3 ✓   4 ✗
5 ✗   6 ✓   7 ✓

15 1 You've got a point there./I see what you mean.
2 No way.
3 Point taken.
4 Fair enough./Point taken./You've got a point there.
5 I see what you mean./you've got a point there.
6 Me neither./Point taken./Fair enough.
7 It's just not on./No way.

Unit 2

1 A Balance Sheet (UK) is the same as a Statement of Financial Position (US). A Profit and Loss Statement (UK) is a Statement of Earnings (US).

2 1 consolidated affiliates
2 retained earnings
3 current receivables
4 common stock
5 total liabilities
6 accumulated gains
7 intangible assets

a intangible assets
b consolidated affiliates
c total liabilities
d common stock
e current receivables
f retained earnings
g accumulated gains

page 17

4 23.56   c   twenty-three point five six

10,001   c   ten thousand and one

£63.30   b   sixty-three pounds and thirty pence

d   sixty-three pounds thirty

5,400,342   c   five million, four hundred thousand, three hundred and forty-two

€45,638   a   forty-five thousand, six hundred and thirty-eight euros

1999   a   nineteen ninety-nine (year)

d   one nine nine nine (if part of a phone number, for example)

2003   b   two double oh three (if a room number or part of a phone number, for example)

c   two thousand and three (year)

page 18

6 1 f (also a or d)   5 a (also d or f)

2 b   6 e

3 h   7 g

4 d (also f)   8 c

page 19

8 1b   average interest rate

2g   earnings per share

3d   return on equity

4f   debt/equity ratio

5a   gross profit margin

6e   inventory turnover

7c   price/earnings ratio

page 20

9 1 to pay   5 to indicate

2 to compare   6 to expand

3 to calculate   7 performance

4 expectation

a expecting

b predict

c calculation(s)

d performed

e expansion

f pay

10 1 over   4 got

2 just   5 questions

3 ask   6 that

11 EPS 2002 - 1.23

EPS 2001 - 1.14

Inv turnover 2002 - 8.32

Inv turnover 2001 - 8.38

Working cap 2002 - 0.75

Working cap 2001 - 0.78

Unit 3

page 22

Start-up   1 income   5 property

2 sales   6 value added

3 inheritance   7 excise

4 corporate

page 23

2 1 straight line   4 hours of use

2 sum-of-the-years'-digits   5 unit of production

3 declining balance

page 24

4 1 interest expenses

2 operating profit

3 prepare an interim tax return

4 the taxation expense we include in the P&L

5 record it as a net deferred tax asset or liability on the balance sheet

5 1 f   2 e   3 d   4 a

5 c   6 g   7 b

page 25

6 1 clarify   4 basically

2 mean   5 depends

3 exactly   6 so

page 26

8 1 g   2 f   3 h   4 d

5 a   6 e   7 b   8 c

9 1 increase   5 exempt

2 bracket   6 breaks

3 exile   7 property

4 abolish   8 return

10 They cannot agree and decide that Uta should make a submission and send it to the IRS office so that her arguments can be considered in detail.

page 27

11 1 to upgrade   4 regulations

2 submission   5 to capitalize

3 interpretation   6 definition

12 *Possible answers:*

1 I'm afraid I can't agree with your comments. I'm sorry but they (just) don't make much sense.

2 I'm sorry, but this conversation … Could you please call me … ?

3 I'm sorry but I disagree … I'm afraid that's not (quite) right.

4 Excuse me, but I think there may be a problem with your idea.

5 Your calculations seem to be full of mistakes.

6 It appears that you don't have the necessary experience to …

page 28

14

	1			2		3						
	S	U	B	M	I	S	S	I	O	N		

Crossword grid:

```
      1S U B M I S S I O N
         N     U
      4C H  5B U D G E T        6
 7D A A E  E          X         9
 8T E M P O R A R Y   E    I
   F  I  T  A  10P  R  N
   E  T  A  C  R  M  T
   R  A  N  T  O  P  E
   R  L     11S C R A P V A L U E
   E  E        I         S
   D           S         T
          12P R O F I T
                O
             13E A R N I N G S
```

Across answers: SUBMISSION, BUDGET, TEMPORARY, SCRAPVALUE, PROFIT, EARNINGS

Unit 4

page 29

Start up The following fall within the normal obligations of auditors: 1, 2, 3, 5, 7, 10, 11

page 30

1 1 False: Klaus wanted to speak to Janet and called her (and left a message).
2 True
3 False: Klaus disagrees. He says the costs were necessary for the upgrade.
4 True
5 True
6 True

page 31

2 1 b   2 a   3 b   4 b
   5 a   6 a   7 b

3 *Janet*   Hendley and Sanderson. Janet Hendley speaking.
Klaus   Hi Janet. It's Klaus.
Janet   Hi Klaus. How's it going?
Klaus   Not too bad. Our latest sales figures are quite good so the boss is happy.
Janet   Good to hear.
Klaus   Listen, Janet. I'm just calling to find out if you've had a chance to look at those capitalization of costs yet. You know – our machine upgrades?
Janet   Yes, yes. Actually, we had a meeting this morning. I was just about to send you an email. You'll be glad to hear that the partners have agreed with your proposal.
Klaus   That's great. It'll really help.
Janet   Glad to be of assistance.
Klaus   Erm. One other thing. There are some other things I'd like to go over with you, but I'd prefer to do it in person, not over the phone. Could you come by the office next week sometime? Tuesday, say?

Janet   Tuesday? No, sorry, I'm afraid I'm busy on Tuesday. What about Wednesday morning? At, say, 9 am?
Klaus   Yes, that sounds good, Wednesday at 9. So, Janet, I'll see you then. Have a good weekend.
Janet   Yes, you too. Bye.
Klaus   Bye.

page 33

6 1 a   2 c   3 j   4 b   5 f
   6 d   7 g   8 h   9 i   10 e

7 1 rose   3 decreased
   2 stable   4 up

Unit 5

page 35

Start-up The statements are all true.

1 Possible reports are:
   a Cost per customer report, with allocation of indirect costs to each customer, together with listing of direct costs which can be attributed to each customer.
   b Profit per customer report, ordered on the size of the orders of the customers, with the income made from each customer, and also with the costs from the first report.
   c Employee costs – maybe based on cost centres, with indirect costs attributed to each employee, together with direct costs, such as salary and benefits.
   d Overhead cost allocation – including report on the basis used, listing of all the costs considered, and summarized against the products made by the company.

page 36

2 1 allocation   5 information
   2 complete   6 production/product
   3 cost   7 profitable
   4 employee   8 sale

   a employ   e profit
   b information   f allocated
   c produces/sell   g complete/produce
   d costly   h sales

3 1 False   4 True   7 False
   2 True   5 False   8 False
   3 True   6 False

page 38

4 1 d   2 g   3 h   4 e
   5 b   6 f   7 c   8 a

6 1 b   2 e   3 f   4 a
   5 d   6 c

page 39

7 R&D Director   Simon
Marketing Director   Peter
Managing Director   Beate
Finance Director   Sally
Investment Director   Gavin
Secretary   Per

page 40

8 1 next item   5 cut back
    2 economic conditions   6 hard times
    3 investment plan   7 middle term
    4 negative outlook   8 capital markets

9 *stating objectives:*
    1   We have to make a decision today about …
    4   What I want to look at is …
    13 Our aim today is to …

asking for contributions:
    3   Anything to add, Harry?
    15 Sally?

moving on:
    9   Shall we move on to the next item?
    11 I'd like to move on if I may.
    12 Perhaps we could discuss that at lunch?

Dealing with communication problems:
    2   So, in other words …
    5   Can you say that again?
    6   You *did* say the 24th, didn't you?
    8   What I'm saying is …
    14 I didn't quite catch that.

Summarizing:
    7   Let me just go over what we have agreed.
    10 To sum up then, …

Unit 6

page 42

Start-up *Possible answers:*
• What is the profitability of the company over the last years, and has it been stable?
• How experienced is the workforce, and how good are their English skills?
• How modern are the machines and working sites of the company?

page 43

2 a acquisition   e invest
   b agree   f legislation
   c consider   g think
   d discussion   h utilize

   1 think   5 invest
   2 investment   6 legislation
   3 acquire   7 discuss
   4 agreement   8 thoughts

3 Hermann is probably the CFO of the subsidiary.

page 44

1 False: Dieter is the head of the company and Hermann is probably the CFO there.
2 False: The British company hasn't agreed to the plan yet.
3 True
4 True
5 True
6 False: He/She doesn't mention this in the email.
7 False: He/She hasn't given a deadline but will be away in the first two weeks of December.

4 1 financial instruments   4 goodwill
    2 taxation system   5 leased products
    3 income statements   6 inventory

page 45

6 She is probably a cross cultural trainer, or an academic working in the field of cross culture.

    1 Intercultural issues facing enterprises with cross-border interests
    2 General issues faced by managers, some issues in more detail, ways to approach problems to create successful international teams
    3 Management should not ignore intercultural factors.

page 46

7 1 If you don't mind, I would prefer to answer any questions you may have at the end.
    2 I will now be happy to take any questions.
    3 There'll be three parts to my presentation.
    4 I'll start with a short description of the general issues.
    5 Then we'll look at some of the issues in more detail.
    6 Finally we'll look at how you can create successful international teams.
    7 There's no need to take notes unless you really want to.

9 1 goodwill   3 takeover   5 acquisition
    2 channels   4 overseas   6 inventory

    hidden word = **invest**

page 49

Test yourself!

Across		Down	
3	amortization	1	consolidation
5	depreciation	2	inventory
7	preliminary	4	overhead
9	property	6	tax exile
11	payroll	8	dividends
13	auditor	10	creative
15	liabilities	12	acquisition
19	revenue	14	transaction
20	upgrade	16	creditor
22	balance	17	purchase
23	intangible	18	subsidiary
26	receivables	21	goodwill
		24	lease
		25	assets

A–Z wordlist

A

to **abolish** [əˈbɒlɪʃ]	abschaffen, streichen
absolutely [ˈæbsəluːtli]	absolut, völlig
to **accelerate** [əkˈseləreɪt]	beschleunigen
accepted [əkˈseptɪd]	akzeptiert
access [ˈækses]	Zugang, Zugriff
accompanying [əˈkʌmpəniɪŋ]	beiliegend, beigefügt
accordance, in ~ with [ɪn əˈkɔːdəns wɪð]	entsprechend, gemäß, in Übereinstimmung mit
according to [əˈkɔːdɪŋ tə]	laut, nach
accordingly [əˈkɔːdɪŋli]	(dem)entsprechend
accountant [əˈkaʊntənt]	(Bilanz-)Buchhalter/in, Wirtschaftsprüfer/in
accounting [əˈkaʊntɪŋ]	Finanz-, Rechnungswesen, Bilanzierung
accounting principles [əˌkaʊntɪŋ ˈprɪnsəplz]	Bilanzierungsrichtlinien
accounts [əˈkaʊnts]	Bücher, Buchhaltungsunterlagen
accounts payable [əˌkaʊnts ˈpeɪəbl]	Verbindlichkeiten, Kreditoren-konten
accrued [əˈkruːd]	aufgelaufen
accumulated gains [əˌkjuːmjəleɪtɪd ˈgeɪnz]	Gewinnvortrag
accumulated losses [əˌkjuːmjəleɪtɪd ˈlɒsɪz]	Verlustvortrag
accurate [ˈækjərət]	genau, (zu)treffend
to **acquire** [əˈkwaɪə]	erwerben, akquirieren
acquisition cost [ˌækwɪˈzɪʃn kɒst]	Anschaffungskosten
actually [ˈæktʃuəli]	eigentlich, tatsächlich
adequate [ˈædɪkwət]	ausreichend
advance, in ~ [ɪn ədˈvɑːns]	im Voraus
to **advise** [ədˈvaɪz]	beraten
to **affect** [əˈfekt]	beeinflussen
to **afford** [əˈfɔːd]	(es) sich leisten (können)
aforementioned [əˌfɔːˈmenʃənd]	oben genannt
agreement [əˈgriːmənt]	Vertrag, Vereinbarung
allegation [ˌæləˈgeɪʃn]	Behauptung, Beschuldigung
to **allocate** [ˈæləkeɪt]	zuweisen, verrechnen
allocation [ˌæləˈkeɪʃn]	Zuweisung, Kontierung
to **allow** [əˈlaʊ]	erlauben, gestatten, (zu)lassen
amortization [əˌmɔːtaɪˈzeɪʃn]	Amortisation, Abschreibung
annual report [ˌænjuəl rɪˈpɔːt]	Jahresabschluss, -bericht
annuity [əˈnjuːəti]	Annuität, Jahreseinkommen
anticipated [ænˈtɪsɪpeɪtɪd]	erwartet
apparently [əˈpærəntli]	offensichtlich, anscheinend
approach [əˈprəʊtʃ]	Methode, Herangehen(sweise)
to **arise** [əˈraɪz]	entstehen, sich ergeben
to **assess** [əˈses]	einschätzen, begutachten
assets [ˈæsets]	Aktiva, Vermögen(swerte)
assistance [əˈsɪstəns]	Hilfe(stellung), Unterstützung
to **associate** [əˈsəʊʃieɪt]	verbinden, in Verbindung bringen
associated company [əˌsəʊʃieɪtɪd ˈkʌmpəni]	Schwesterfirma, Beteiligungs-gesellschaft
to **assume** [əˈsjuːm]	annehmen, glauben
assumption [əˈsʌmpʃn]	Annahme, Voraussetzung
assurance [əˈʃʊərəns]	Sicherheit, Gewissheit
to **attract** [əˈtrækt]	anlocken, gewinnen
audit [ˈɔːdɪt]	Bilanz-, Rechnungs-, Buchprüfung
average cost [ˌævərɪdʒ ˈkɒst]	Durchschnittskosten
average interest rate [ˌævərɪdʒ ˈɪntrəst reɪt]	durchschnittliche/r Zinssatz, -rate
aware [əˈweə]	bewusst

B

balance sheet [ˈbæləns ʃiːt]	Bilanz(bogen), Rechnungs-abschluss
basic earnings per share [ˌbeɪsɪk ˈɜːnɪŋz pə ʃeə]	Gewinn je Aktie
bean counter [ˈbiːn kaʊntə]	Erbsenzähler/in

to **benefit** [ˈbenɪfɪt]	nutzen
board meeting [ˈbɔːd miːtɪŋ]	Aufsichtsratssitzung
board of accountancy [bɔːd əv əˈkaʊntənsi]	Finanzbehörde
board of directors [ˌbɔːd əv dəˈrektəz]	Aufsichtsrat, Vorstand
body [ˈbɒdi]	Amt, Behörde
book value [ˈbʊk væljuː]	Netto-, Bilanz-, Buchwert
bookkeeper [ˈbʊkkiːpə]	Buchhalter/in
borrowing [ˈbɒrəʊɪŋ]	Geld-, Kreditaufnahme
breakdown [ˈbreɪkdaʊn]	Aufteilung, Aufschlüsselung
to **brief** [briːf]	einweisen, instruieren
budgeting [ˈbʌdʒɪtɪŋ]	Geschäfts-, Finanzplanung
to **burden** [ˈbɜːdn]	belasten

C

to **calculate** [ˈkælkjuleɪt]	kalkulieren, berechnen
calculation [ˌkælkjuˈleɪʃn]	Berechnung, Rechenart
capital expenditure [ˌkæpɪtl ɪkˈspendɪtʃə]	Kapital-, Investitionsaufwand
capital goods and services [ˌkæpɪtl ˌgʊdz ən ˈsɜːvɪsɪz]	Kapitalgüter und -dienstleistun-gen
capital market [ˈkæpɪtl mɑːkɪt]	Kapitalmarkt
capitalization of costs [ˌkæpɪtəlaɪˈzeɪʃn əv kɒsts]	Kapitalisierung der Kosten
to **capitalize** [ˈkæpɪtəlaɪz]	kapitalisieren
case study [ˈkeɪs stʌdi]	Fallstudie
cash cow [ˈkæʃ kaʊ]	Milchkuh
cash flow statement [ˈkæʃ fləʊ steɪtmənt]	Kapitalflussrechnung
cash on delivery [ˌkæʃ ɒn dɪˈlɪvəri]	Nachnahme, Barzahlung bei Lieferung
certification [ˌsɜːtɪfɪˈkeɪʃn]	Beglaubigung, Zulassung
certified public accountant (CPA) [ˌsɜːtɪfaɪd ˌpʌblɪk əˈkaʊntənt]	vereidigte/r Wirtschaftsprüfer/in
chairperson [ˈtʃeəpɜːsn]	Vorsitzende/r, Moderator/in
charges [ˈtʃɑːdʒɪz]	Gebühren, Spesen, (Un-)Kosten
chartered accountant [ˌtʃɑːtəd əˈkaʊntənt]	vereidigte/r Wirtschaftsprüfer/in, Buchhalter/in, Steuerberater/in
chief financial controller [ˌtʃiːf faɪˌnænʃl kənˈtrəʊlə]	Leiter/in der Finanzprüfung
to **clarify** [ˈklærəfaɪ]	(auf)klären, deutlich machen
classification [ˌklæsɪfɪˈkeɪʃn]	Klassifizierung, Einstufung
clue, to not have a ~ [kluː]	keine Ahnung haben
to **collapse** [kəˈlæps]	zusammenbrechen, scheitern
commercial [kəˈmɜːʃl]	Handels-, Wirtschafts-
to **commit fraud** [kəˌmɪt ˈfrɔːd]	Betrug begehen
commitment [kəˈmɪtmənt]	Einsatz, Engagement
common stock [ˌkɒmən ˈstɒk]	Stammaktie
common stockholder [ˌkɒmən ˈstɒkhəʊldə]	Stammaktionär/in
compliance [kəmˈplaɪəns]	Einhaltung, Befolgung
comprehensive [ˌkɒmprɪˈhensɪv]	umfassend
to **conclude** [kənˈkluːd]	schließen, folgern
condition [kənˈdɪʃn]	Bedingung
to **conduct** [kənˈdʌkt]	durchführen
confidentiality [ˌkɒnfɪˌdenʃiˈæləti]	Vertraulichkeit
to **conform** [kənˈfɔːm]	entsprechen
conformity, in ~ with [ɪn kənˈfɔːməti wɪð]	in Übereinstimmung mit
conglomerate [kənˈglɒmərət]	Großkonzern
to **consider** [kənˈsɪdə]	erwägen, prüfen
considerable [kənˈsɪdərəbl]	beträchtlich, beachtlich
consideration [kənˌsɪdəˈreɪʃn]	Erwägung, Überlegung
to **consist of** [kənˈsɪst əv]	bestehen aus
consolidated [kɒnˈsɒlɪdeɪtɪd]	konsolidiert, vereinigt
consolidated affiliate [kənˌsɒlɪdeɪtɪd əˈfɪliət]	konsolidiertes Verbundunter-nehmen

consolidation [kən‚sɒlɪ'deɪʃn]	Festigung, Konsolidierung	
consulting [kən'sʌltɪŋ]	(Unternehmens-)Beratung	
consumer [kən'sju:mə]	Verbraucher/in	
contract ['kɒntrækt]	Vertrag	
contractual [kən'træktʃuəl]	vertraglich	
contribution [‚kɒntrɪ'bju:ʃn]	Beitrag	
to convince [kən'vɪns]	überzeugen	
corporation [‚kɔ:pə'reɪʃn]	(Aktien-)Gesellschaft, Kapital-gesellschaft	
cost accounting ['kɒst əkaʊntɪŋ]	Kostenrechnung, Kalkulation, Betriebsabrechnung	
cost effective [‚kɒst ɪ'fektɪv]	kostenwirksam, -effektiv	
count up [‚kaʊnt 'ʌp]	zusammenzählen, addieren	
creative accounting [kri‚eɪtɪv ə'kaʊntɪŋ]	kreative Buchführung	
creditors ['kredɪtəz]	Gläubiger, Kreditoren(konten)	
critical ['krɪtɪkl]	entscheidend	
criteria [kraɪ'tɪəriə]	Kriterien, Kennzeichen	
to cruise along [kru:z ə'lɒŋ]	langsam umherfahren	
cumulative effect [‚kju:mjələtɪv ɪ'fekt]	gesteigerte Wirkung	
currency translation adjustment [‚kʌrənsi træns‚leɪʃn ə'dʒʌstmənt]	Währungsausgleich	
current ['kʌrənt]	aktuell, gegenwärtig	
current assets [‚kʌrənt 'æsets]	(kurzfristige) Umlaufvermögen	
current costs and expenses [‚kʌrənt kɒsts ənd ɪk'spensɪz]	laufende Kosten und Unkosten	
current liabilities [‚kʌrənt ‚laɪə'bɪlətiz]	kurzfristige (oder laufende) Verbindlichkeiten	
current receivables [‚kʌrənt rɪ'si:vəblz]	Umlaufvermögen	
currently ['kʌrəntli]	momentan, zurzeit	
to cut back [‚kʌt 'bæk]	kürzen, zurückschrauben	
cycle ['saɪkl]	Zyklus, Kreislauf	

D

debt [det]	Schuld(en)
debt/asset ratio [‚det ‚æset 'reɪʃiəʊ]	Verhältnis der Schuld- zu den Aktivposten
debt/equity ratio [‚det ‚ekwəti 'reɪʃiəʊ]	Verhältnis der Passiva zum Eigenkapital
declared [dɪ'kleəd]	erklärt, ausgeschüttet
declining balance [dɪ‚klaɪnɪŋ 'bæləns]	degressive Abschreibung
to defend [dɪ'fend]	verteidigen
deferred [dɪ'fɜ:d]	aufgeschoben, ausgesetzt
deferred income tax(es) [dɪ‚fɜ:d 'ɪnkʌm tæksɪz]	Einkommen(s)steuervoraus-zahlung(en)
denominator [dɪ'nɒmɪneɪtə]	Nenner
dependent on [dɪ'pendənt ɒn]	abhängig von
to depreciate [dɪ'pri:ʃieɪt]	abschreiben, an Wert verlieren
depreciation [dɪ‚pri:ʃi'eɪʃn]	Wertminderung, -berichtigung, Abschreibung
to determine [dɪ'tɜ:mɪn]	bestimmen, feststellen
deviation [‚di:vi'eɪʃn]	Abweichung
to differ ['dɪfə]	sich unterscheiden
diluted earnings per share [daɪ‚lu:tɪd 'ɜ:nɪŋz pə ʃeə]	Gewinn je Aktie einschließlich aller Umtauschrechte
disappointing [‚dɪsə'pɔɪntɪŋ]	enttäuschend
to disclose [dɪs'kləʊz]	offen legen, anzeigen
disclosure [dɪs'kləʊʒə]	Offenlegung, Angabe
discounted cash flow [dɪs‚kaʊntɪd 'kæʃ fləʊ]	diskontierte Dividendenaus-schüttung, bereinigter Gewinn
disposition [‚dɪspə'zɪʃn]	Veräußerung
to distribute [dɪ'strɪbju:t]	verteilen
distribution channel [‚dɪstrɪ'bju:ʃn tʃænl]	Vertriebsweg
dividends payable [‚dɪvɪdendz 'peɪəbl]	fällige Dividenden
domestic [də'mestɪk]	inländisch, (ein)heimisch
drop [drɒp]	Rückgang
due diligence [dju: 'dɪlɪdʒəns]	erforderliche oder ange-messene Sorgfalt
due, to be ~ to [bi 'dju: tə]	resultieren aus

E

earnings per share ['ɜ:nɪŋz pə ʃeə]	Aktienrendite, Gewinn je Aktie
effect [ɪ'fekt]	(Aus-)Wirkung
effectively [ɪ'fektɪvli]	effektiv, tatsächlich
efficiency [ɪ'fɪʃnsi]	Leistungsfähigkeit
efficient [ɪ'fɪʃnt]	effizient, (leistungs)fähig
to employ [ɪm'plɔɪ]	anstellen, beschäftigen
employee [ɪm'plɔɪi:]	Arbeitnehmer/in, Beschäftigte/r
to enable [ɪ'neɪbl]	(es) ermöglichen, befähigen
to enact [ɪ'nækt]	erlassen
to encourage [ɪn'kʌrɪdʒ]	fördern, unterstützen
enterprise ['entəpraɪz]	Unternehmen
equity ['ekwəti]	Eigenkapital, (industrielles) Wertpapier
equivalent [ɪ'kwɪvələnt]	Entsprechung, Gegenwert
to establish [ɪ'stæblɪʃ]	festlegen
estimate ['estɪmət]	(Ein-)Schätzung
estimated scrap value [‚estɪmeɪtɪd 'skræp vælju:]	geschätzter Schrottwert
to evaluate [ɪ'væljueɪt]	(ein)schätzen, (be)werten
evaluation [ɪ‚vælju'eɪʃn]	(Ein-)Schätzung, Bewertung
event, in the ~ of [ɪn ði ɪ'vent əv]	im Falle eines
ever-increasing [‚evər ɪn'kri:sɪŋ]	ständig steigend
to exclude [ɪk'sklu:d]	ausschließen
to expand [ɪk'spænd]	expandieren, sich vergrößern
expectation [‚ekspek'teɪʃn]	Erwartung
expenditure [ɪk'spendɪtʃə]	Ausgabe(n), (Un-)Kosten
to expense [ɪk'spens]	als Kosten buchen
expense [ɪk'spens]	Kosten, (einzelne) Ausgabe
expertise [‚eksp3:'ti:z]	Sachkenntnis
to express [ɪk'spres]	ausdrücken
extensively [ɪk'stensɪvli]	umfassend
external accounts [ɪk‚st3:nl ə'kaʊnts]	ausländische Bilanzen
external auditor [ɪk‚st3:nl 'ɔ:dɪtə]	außerbetriebliche/r Wirtschafts-prüfer/in
extremely [ɪk'stri:mli]	äußerst, außerordentlich

F

to face [feɪs]	rechnen müssen mit
failure ['feɪljə]	Misserfolg, Scheitern
fair value [feə 'vælju:]	angemessener Wert
fee [fi:]	Gebühr, Honorar
to fill sb in on [fɪl 'ɪn ɒn]	jdn informieren über
finance director [‚faɪnæns də'rektə]	Finanzdirektor/in
finance ['faɪnæns]	Finanz(en), Finanz-
to finance ['faɪnæns]	finanzieren
financial director [faɪ‚nænʃl də'rektə]	Finanzdirektor/in
financial instrument [faɪ‚nænʃl 'ɪnstrəmənt]	Kreditinstrument
financial statement [faɪ‚nænʃl 'steɪtmənt]	Vermögensaufstellung, Finanz-status
financing activities [faɪ‚nænsɪŋ æk'tɪvətiz]	Finanzierungen
financing receivables [faɪnænsɪŋ rɪ'si:vəblz]	Forderungen aus Krediten
first in first out [‚f3:st ɪn ‚f3:st 'aʊt]	wie eingetroffen
fixed assets [fɪkst 'æsets]	Sachanlagevermögen
fluctuation [‚flʌktʃu'eɪʃn]	Schwankung
to get a foothold [get ə 'fʊthəʊld]	Fuß fassen
forecast ['fɔ:kɑ:st]	Vorhersage, Prognose
fund [fʌnd]	Fonds
funding ['fʌndɪŋ]	Finanzierung
fuss [fʌs]	Aufhebens, Theater

G

gain [geɪn]	Gewinn
to gather evidence [‚gæðər 'evɪdəns]	Beweise sammeln
gearing ['gɪərɪŋ]	Fremdkapitalaufnahme
goodwill [‚gʊd'wɪl]	Geschäftswert, Firmenwert
to govern ['gʌvn]	bestimmen, regeln
gradual ['grædʒuəl]	allmählich

gross (profit) margin   Bruttogewinnspanne
[ˌɡrəʊs (ˈprɒfɪt) ˈmɑːdʒɪn]
growth [ɡrəʊθ]   Wachstum
to **guarantee** [ˌɡærənˈtiː]   garantieren
guilty, to be ~ of sth [ˈɡɪlti]   schuldig sein an (einer Sache)

H
hang on [ˌhæŋ ˈɒn]   warte!
high flyer [ˌhaɪ ˈflaɪə]   Senkrechtstarter/in
hospitality [ˌhɒspɪˈtæləti]   Gastfreundschaft, -lichkeit
to **hover** [ˈhɒvə]   kreisen, sich bewegen

I
impact [ˈɪmpækt]   (Aus-)Wirkung, Effekt
to **impair** [ɪmˈpeə]   schädigen, behindern
implication [ˌɪmplɪˈkeɪʃn]   Auswirkung
to **impose** [ɪmˈpəʊz]   auferlegen, erheben
impressive [ɪmˈpresɪv]   eindrucksvoll
improper [ɪmˈprɒpə]   unzulässig
to **improve** [ɪmˈpruːv]   verbessern
income [ˈɪnkʌm]   Einkommen
income statement   Gewinn- und Verlust-
[ˈɪnkʌm steɪtmənt]   rechnung
income tax [ˈɪnkʌm tæks]   Einkommen(s)steuer
indication [ˌɪndɪˈkeɪʃn]   Angabe
insurance liabilities   Verbindlichkeiten aus
[ɪnˈʃʊərəns ˌlaɪəˈbɪlətiz]   Versicherungen
insurance loss [ɪnˈʃʊərəns lɒs]   Versicherungsschaden
insurance receivables   Forderungen aus Versiche-
[ɪnˈʃʊərəns rɪˈsiːvəblz]   rungen
intangible assets   immaterielle(s)
[ɪnˈtændʒəbl ˈæsets]   Vermögen(swerte)
intangibles [ɪnˈtændʒəblz]   immaterielle Anlagewert
interest [ˈɪntrəst]   Zins(en)
interim [ˈɪntərɪm]   einstweilig, vorläufig
internal auditor [ɪnˌtɜːnl ˈɔːdɪtə]   betriebseigene/r Wirtschafts-
   prüfer/in
Internal Revenue Service (AE)   Einkommensteuerbehörde
[ɪnˌtɜːnl ˈrevənjuː ˈsɜːvɪs]
to **interpret** [ɪnˈtɜːprɪt]   interpretieren, auslegen
inventory [ˈɪnvəntri]   Waren- und Lagerbestand
inventory turnover   Lagerumschlag
[ˌɪnvəntri ˈtɜːnəʊvə]
investment [ɪnˈvestmənt]   Investition, Anlage
investment director   Investitionsleiter/in
[ɪnˌvestmənt dəˈrektə]
investment security   (erstklassiges) Anlagepapier
[ɪnˌvestmənt sɪˈkjʊərəti]
investor [ɪnˈvestə]   Investor/in, (Kapital-)Anleger/in
item [ˈaɪtəm]   Punkt, Posten

J
to **justify** [ˈdʒʌstɪfaɪ]   rechtfertigen, verteidigen

K
to **kid** [kɪd]   Witze machen, scherzen
knowledge [ˈnɒlɪdʒ]   Wissen, Kenntnis(se)

L
last in first out [ˌlɑːst ˈɪn ˌfɜːst ˈaʊt]   die älteste Anträge zuerst
to **launch** [lɔːntʃ]   auf den Markt bringen, einführen
layman [ˈleɪmən]   Laie
leasing [ˈliːsɪŋ]   Leasing, (Ver-)Mieten
to **legislate** [ˈledʒɪsleɪt]   Gesetze erlassen
legislation [ˌledʒɪsˈleɪʃn]   Gesetze, gesetzliche Regelung(en)
legitimate [lɪˈdʒɪtɪmət]   legitim, berechtigt
leverage [ˈliːvərɪdʒ]   Fremdkapitalaufnahme
liabilities [ˌlaɪəˈbɪlətiz]   Verbindlichkeiten, Schulden,
   Passiva
liability [ˌlaɪəˈbɪləti]   Verpflichtung
liable [ˈlaɪəbl]   verpflichtet, verantwortlich
loan [ləʊn]   Kredit, Darlehen
local authority [ˌləʊkl ɔːˈθɒrəti]   Kommunalbehörde
loose, to be let ~ [bi let ˈluːs]   losgelassen werden

M
to **maintain** [meɪnˈteɪn]   bewahren, einhalten
maintenance [ˈmeɪntənəns]   Wartung, Instandhaltung
management account   Geschäftskonto
[ˈmænɪdʒmənt əkaʊnt]

management accounting   Rechnungswesen für Betriebs-
[ˈmænɪdʒmənt əkaʊntɪŋ]   führung, internes Rechnungswesen
mandatory [ˈmændətəri]   obligatorisch, zwingend,
   verbindlich
manufacturing costs   Herstellkosten
[ˌmænjuˈfæktərɪŋ kɒsts]
market capitalization   Kapitalisierungsmarkt(wert)
[ˌmɑːkɪt ˌkæpɪtəlaɪˈzeɪʃn]
market price [ˈmɑːkɪt praɪs]   Marktpreis
market value [ˌmɑːkɪt ˈvæljuː]   Marktwert
mark-up margin   Handelsspanne
[ˌmɑːkʌp ˈmɑːdʒɪn]
material [məˈtɪəriəl]   relevant, wesentlich
maturity [məˈtʃʊərəti]   Fälligkeit
mechanics [mɪˈkænɪks]   Mechanismus, Ablauf, Abwicklung
mechanism [ˈmekənɪzəm]   Mechanismus
to **mention** [ˈmenʃn]   erwähnen, nennen
merger [ˈmɜːdʒə]   Fusion, Firmenzusammenschluss
minority interest   Minderheitsbeteiligung
[maɪˌnɒrəti ˈɪntrəst]
to **mislead** [ˌmɪsˈliːd]   irreführen, in die Irre führen
misleading [ˌmɪsˈliːdɪŋ]   irreführend
misstatement [ˌmɪsˈsteɪtmənt]   Falschaussage
to **move on** [ˌmuːv ˈɒn]   weitergehen, fortfahren

N
negotiation [nɪˌɡəʊʃiˈeɪʃn]   Verhandlung
net [net]   netto, Netto-
net assets [ˌnet ˈæsets]   Reinvermögen
net earnings [ˌnet ˈɜːnɪŋz]   Nettoverdienst, Reingewinn,
   Einkünfte
non-existent [ˌnɒn ɪɡˈzɪstənt]   nicht vorhanden
not-for-profit [ˌnɒt fə ˈprɒfɪt]   gemeinnützig
numerator [ˈnjuːməreɪtə]   Zähler

O
objective [əbˈdʒektɪv]   Ziel, Zweck
obligation [ˌɒblɪˈɡeɪʃn]   Verpflichtung, Verbindlichkeit
to **obtain** [əbˈteɪn]   erhalten, erlangen, gewinnen
off-balance-sheet accounting   Buchführung ohne Bilanzauf-
[ˌɒf ˈbæləns ʃiːt əˈkaʊntɪŋ]   stellung
offset [ˈɒfset]   ausgleichen, absetzen
operating activities   Betriebstätigkeit
[ˌɒpəreɪtɪŋ ækˈtɪvətiz]
operating profit [ˈɒpəreɪtɪŋ prɒfɪt]   Betriebsgewinn
operations [ˌɒpəˈreɪʃnz]   Geschäftstätigkeit
opportunity [ˌɒpəˈtjuːnəti]   Gelegenheit, Chance, Möglichkeit
ordinary share capital   Stammkapital
[ˌɔːdnri ˈʃeə kæpɪtl]
outlook [ˈaʊtlʊk]   Sicht, Auffassung, Ausblick
outside parties [ˌaʊtsaɪd ˈpɑːtiz]   Außenstehende
overhead expenses   allgemeine Unkosten
[ˌəʊvəhed ɪkˈspensɪz]
overseas [ˌəʊvəˈsiːz]   ausländisch, im Ausland
to **overstate** [ˌəʊvəˈsteɪt]   übertreiben, zu hoch angeben

P
parent company   Mutterfirma
[ˌpeərənt ˈkʌmpəni]
pay cut [ˈpeɪ kʌt]   Gehaltskürzung
to **pay off** [ˌpeɪ ˈɒf]   ab(be)zahlen, zurückzahlen,
   tilgen
payment [ˈpeɪmənt]   Bezahlung, Zahlung
payroll tax [ˈpeɪrəʊl tæks]   Lohnsteuer
peer [pɪə]   Gleichgestellte/r, Kollege/-gin
performance [pəˈfɔːməns]   Vorstellung, Geschäftsgebaren
periodic [ˌpɪəriˈɒdɪk]   regelmäßig
personnel [ˌpɜːsəˈnel]   Personal
pessimistically [ˌpesɪˈmɪstɪkli]   pessimistisch
petty cash [ˌpeti ˈkæʃ]   Portokasse
plant [plɑːnt]   (Industrie-)Anlage
policyholder [ˈpɒləsihəʊldə]   Versicherte/r, Versicherungs-
   nehmer/in
to **postpone** [pəˈspəʊn]   verschieben
to **predict** [prɪˈdɪkt]   vorhersagen
prediction [prɪˈdɪkʃn]   Vorhersage

preliminary report	Vorbericht	
[prɪˌlɪmɪnəri rɪˈpɔːt]		
price/earnings ratio	Kurs-Gewinn-Verhältnis	
[ˌpraɪs ˌɜːnɪŋz ˈreɪʃiəʊ]		
pricing policy [ˈpraɪsɪŋ pɒləsi]	Preispolitik	
principal [ˈprɪnsəpl]	Haupt-; Grundsatz, Prinzip	
profit and loss account	Gewinn- und Verlustrechnung	
[ˌprɒfɪt ən ˈlɒs əkaʊnt]		
profitability [ˌprɒfɪtəˈbɪləti]	Rentabilität, Einträglichkeit	
profitable [ˈprɒfɪtəbl]	gewinnbringend, rentabel	
to **promote** [prəˈməʊt]	fördern	
property [ˈprɒpəti]	(Grund-)Besitz, Immobilie(n)	
proportion [prəˈpɔːʃn]	Anteil, Verhältnis	
proposal [prəˈpəʊzl]	Vorschlag, Antrag	
to **prove** [pruːv]	nachweisen	
provided [prəˈvaɪdɪd]	vorausgesetzt	
provision [prəˈvɪʒn]	Rückstellung, -lage, Reserve	
provisional [prəˈvɪʒənl]	provisorisch, vorläufig	
publicly listed [ˈpʌblɪkli ˌlɪstɪd]	öffentlich eingetragenes, börsennotiertes	
publicly traded [ˌpʌblɪkli ˈtreɪdɪd]	an der Börse gehandelt	
to **punch numbers** [pʌntʃ ˈnʌmbəz]	Zahlen eingeben	
purchase price [ˈpɜːtʃəs praɪs]	Einkaufspreis	

Q

qualify [ˈkwɒlɪfaɪ]	(sich) qualifizieren
quantitative [ˈkwɒntɪtətɪv]	quantitativ, mengenmäßig
to **quote** [kwəʊt]	angeben, nennen

R

to **raise capital** [reɪz ˈkæpɪtl]	Kapital beschaffen
ratio [ˈreɪʃiəʊ]	(Wert-)Verhältnis
ratio analysis [ˌreɪʃiəʊ əˈnæləsɪs]	Bilanzanalyse
to **realize** [ˈrɪəlaɪz]	(be)merken, sich bewusst sein
reasonable [ˈriːznəbl]	vernünftig
receivables [rɪˈsiːvəblz]	Forderungen, Außenstände
to **recognize** [ˈrekəgnaɪz]	(an)erkennen
to **reconcile** [ˈrekənsaɪl]	ausgleichen
reconciliation to [ˌrekənˌsɪliˈeɪʃn tə]	Abstimmung auf
to **record** [rɪˈkɔːd]	ver-, aufzeichnen
to **register** [ˈredʒɪstə]	eintragen, anmelden, registrieren
to **regulate** [ˈregjuleɪt]	regeln, regulieren
regulation [ˌregjuˈleɪʃn]	Bestimmung, Verordnung
regulatory authority [ˈregjələtəri ɔːˈθɒrəti]	Aufsichtsbehörde
to **rely on** [rɪˈlaɪ ɒn]	sich verlassen auf
to **remind** [rɪˈmaɪnd]	(jdn an etw) erinnern
to **repay** [rɪˈpeɪ]	tilgen, zurückzahlen
requirement [rɪˈkwaɪəmənt]	Anforderung, Voraussetzung
reserve [rɪˈzɜːv]	Reserve, Rücklage, -stellung
responsibility [rɪˌspɒnsəˈbɪləti]	Verantwortung, Verantwortlichkeit
responsible [rɪˈspɒnsəbl]	verantwortlich
retained earnings [rɪˌteɪnd ˈɜːnɪŋz]	thesaurierter Gewinn, einbehaltene Einkünfte
return on assets [rɪˌtɜːn ɒn ˈæsets]	Anlagenrendite
return on equity [rɪˌtɜːn ɒn ˈekwəti]	(Eigen)Kapitalrendite
to **re-value** [ˌriːˈvæljuː]	neu bewerten
revenues [ˈrevənjuːz]	Einkünfte, Einnahmen
risk-worthy [ˈrɪsk wɜːði]	risikoträchtig
rubbish [ˈrʌbɪʃ]	Unsinn
rule [ruːl]	Vorschrift, Regel

S

sales figures [ˈseɪlz fɪgəz]	Absatzzahlen
sales tax [ˈseɪlz tæks]	Umsatzsteuer
salvage value [ˈsælvɪdʒ væljuː]	Schrottwert
scope [skəʊp]	(Spiel-)Raum
self-generated [ˌselfˈdʒenəreɪtɪd]	selbst erstellt
self-regulation [ˌselfˌregjuˈleɪʃn]	eigene Maßnahmen
share [ʃeə]	(Geschäfts-)Anteil, Aktie
share owner [ˈʃeə əʊnə]	Anteilseigner/in
shareholder [ˈʃeəhəʊldə]	Aktionär/in, Anteilseigner/in
shareholder's equity [ˌʃeəhəʊldəz ˈekwəti]	Eigenkapital
short term assets [ˌʃɔːt tɜːm ˈæsets]	kurzfristige Aktiva, Umlaufvermögen
significant(ly) [sɪgˈnɪfɪkənt(li)]	erheblich, deutlich

sizeable [ˈsaɪzəbl]	beträchtlich	
to **soften** [ˈsɒfn]	abschwächen	
solid [ˈsɒlɪd]	solide, kreditwürdig	
source and application of funds [ˌsɔːs ənd ˌæplɪˈkeɪʃn əv fʌndz]	Kapitalflussrechnung	
source of supply [sɔːs əv səˈplaɪ]	Liefer-, Bezugsquelle	
statement of cash flows [ˌsteɪtmənt əv ˈkæʃ fləʊz]	Kapitalabschlussrechnung, Bruttoertragsanalyse	
statement of earnings [ˌsteɪtmənt əv ˈɜːnɪŋz]	Ertragnisaufstellung, Gewinn- und Verlustrechnung	
statement of financial position [ˌsteɪtmənt əv faɪˌnænʃl pəˈzɪʃn]	Bilanz	
stock exchange [ˈstɒk ɪkstʃeɪndʒ]	(Effekten-, Wertpapier-)Börse	
stringent [ˈstrɪndʒənt]	zwingend, streng	
submission [səbˈmɪʃn]	Eingabe, Antrag	
subsidiary [səbˈsɪdiəri]	Tochter(gesellschaft)	
successive [səkˈsesɪv]	aufeinander folgend	
sufficient [səˈfɪʃnt]	ausreichend, genügend	
to **sum up** [ˌsʌm ˈʌp]	zusammenfassen	
sum-of-the-years' digit [ˌsʌm əv ðə ˌjɪəz ˈdɪdʒɪt]	digitale Abschreibung	
supplemental disclosure [sʌplɪˌmentl dɪsˈkləʊʒə]	ergänzende Angaben	

T

to **take into account** [ˌteɪk ɪntu əˈkaʊnt]	in Betracht ziehen, berücksichtigen
takeover [ˈteɪkəʊvə]	Übernahme
tax accounting [ˈtæks əkaʊntɪŋ]	Steuerbuchhaltung
tax asset [tæks ˈæset]	Ertragsteueranspruch
tax authority [ˌtæks ɔːˈθɒrəti]	Steuerbehörde, Finanzamt
tax avoidance [ˈtæks əvɔɪdəns]	Steuervermeidung
tax bracket [ˈtæks brækɪt]	Steuerklasse, -stufe
tax break [ˈtæks breɪk]	(zeitweilige) Steuerbefreiung, -vergünstigung, -vorteil
tax deductible [ˈtæks dɪˈdʌktəbl]	steuerlich absetzbar, abzugsfähig
tax evasion [ˈtæks ɪveɪʒn]	Steuerhinterziehung
tax exempt [ˌtæks ɪgˈzempt]	steuerfrei
tax exile [ˈtæks eksaɪl]	Steuerflüchtling
tax liability [tæks ˌlaɪəˈbɪləti]	Ertragsteuerverpflichtung
tax return [ˈtæks rɪtɜːn]	Steuererklärung
taxable [ˈtæksəbl]	steuerpflichtig
taxation [tækˈseɪʃn]	Besteuerung, Steuerwesen
taxation expense [tækˌseɪʃn ɪkˈspens]	Steuerausgaben, -Aufwand
term, in the long ~ [ɪn ðə ˈlɒŋ tɜːm]	langfristig, auf lange Sicht
term, in the middle ~ [ɪn ðə ˈmɪdl tɜːm]	mittelfristig
theory, in ~ [ɪn ˈθɪəri]	theoretisch
trademark [ˈtreɪd mɑːk]	Warenzeichen, Handelsmarke
trader [ˈtreɪdə]	(Börsen-)Händler/in, Makler/in
travel expenses [ˈtrævl ɪkspensɪz]	Reisekosten, -spesen
treatment [ˈtriːtmənt]	Behandlung, Umgang
tune, to the ~ of [tjuːn]	in Höhe von

U

undistributed [ˌʌndɪˈstrɪbjuːtɪd]	unverteilt, nicht ausgeschüttet
unrealized [ʌnˈrɪəlaɪzd]	nicht realisiert
to **unsettle** [ʌnˈsetl]	verunsichern
upcoming [ˈʌpkʌmɪŋ]	kommend, bevorstehend, nächst
to **upgrade** [ʌpˈgreɪd]	ausbauen, verbessern
upgrade [ˈʌpgreɪd]	Ausbau, Modernisierung
upwards [ˈʌpwədz]	nach oben, aufwärts
urgent [ˈɜːdʒənt]	dringend, eilig
utilization [ˌjuːtəlaɪˈzeɪʃn]	Verwertung, Verwendung
to **utilize** [ˈjuːtəlaɪz]	einsetzen, (be)nutzen

V

value [ˈvæljuː]	Wert
to **value** [ˈvæljuː]	(ab)schätzen, (be)werten
to **vary** [ˈveəri]	sich unterscheiden, variieren
viable [ˈvaɪəbl]	lebensfähig

W

wealth [welθ]	Reichtum, Vermögen
wear and tear [ˌweər ən ˈteə]	Abnutzung, Verschleiß
working capital [ˌwɜːkɪŋ ˈkæpɪtl]	Betriebs-, Umlaufkapital
to **write off** [ˌraɪt ˈɒf]	abschreiben

Glossary of financial terms

accounts payable
The amounts that a person or organization owes to someone else in the normal daily business.

accounts receivable
The amounts that a person or organization is owed in the normal daily business, ie, excluding loans and liabilities.

acquisition
Another word for purchase. Normally used for very large amounts, such as buildings, factories or another company (verb: to acquire).

affiliate
A person or company which is in some way connected to another.

American Institute of Certified Public Accountants (AICPA)
The professional body of accountants in the USA.

amortization
The process to reduce the value of an intangible asset to zero, over a specified number of years (verb: to amortize).

assets
The things which a person or company owns and which are of value to the owner.

Balance Sheet
A written statement showing 1) the amount of money and property a company has and 2) the money received from shareholders and creditors.

Board (of Directors)
The top management of a company.

branch
The offices of a company which are located in various countries or cities. A branch is not a separate company.

budget
The fixing of the amounts to be spent in the future. Also, the official statement showing these amounts.

capitalization
When a company spends money on something which will last for more than one year. This amount is normally put into the Balance Sheet.

Certified Public Accountant (CPA)
The title given to state recognized accountants in the United States of America.

confidentiality
Not telling others about information which a business partner or client tells you.

consistency principle
The idea that accounts should be prepared on the same basis from one year to the next.

consolidation
The process of including the figures of subsidiaries and affiliates in the accounts of a holding company.

creative accounting
The manipulation of figures in the accounts, designed to give a better result for the company.

creditor
a person or organization to whom money is owed.

debt
An amount which has to be paid to another party. (See also: to service debt.)

deferred
The inclusion in the accounts of amounts which will have to be paid in the future, but which are based on current transactions.

depreciation
The process to reduce the value of an asset to zero, over a specified number of years (verb: to depreciate).

disposition
Another word for the sale of an asset.

dividend
The distribution of the profits of a company to its owners.

due diligence
The process of checking the finances and contracts of a company before the purchase of its assets or shares, to ensure all relevant information has been given.

expenditure
The money spent on buying assets, which will then be included in the Balance Sheet.

to expense
When used as a verb, this word means that an amount of money spent by a company can go directly into the Profit and Loss Statement.

gearing
The proportion of debt and equity ownership in a company or an asset.

Generally Accepted Accounting Principles (GAAP)
These are the rules which accountants are required to follow when preparing financial statements, which are not written into law.

going concern principle
The idea that financial information can only be reported correctly on the basis that the company will be able to operate in the future.

goodwill
The total value of a company minus the net value of the tangible assets.

holding company
The company which owns the shares in all the other companies in a group.

to impair
Used to describe the process of reducing the value of an intangible asset.

Institute of Chartered Accountants in England and Wales (ICAEW)
The professional body of accountants in the United Kingdom.

intangible
Something which has no physical presence, but is only an abstract idea. (Intangible assets, for example, are patents, trademarks or brands.)

International Accounting Standards (IAS)
Currently the International Financial Reporting Standards.

International Accounting Standards Committee (IASC)
The body responsible for the creation of an international set of accounting standards.

International Financial Reporting Standards (IFRS)
The set of standards created to unify accounting practices in the world. Replaced the former International Accounting Standards.

inventory
The goods which a company produces, but which have not yet been sold.

leasing
A legal contract to rent assets from the owner, often over long periods of time and with the possibility to buy the asset at the end of the rental period.

liability
The amount of money or the value of something which a person or organization owes to someone else. For insurance matters, 'liability' means the responsibility to pay the costs of an accident.

liquidation
The dissolving of a company which can no longer pay its bills.

to loan
When one party gives another an amount of money which will be paid back at a later date (noun: loan).

margin
The difference between the sales value and the direct costs of producing an item.

matching principle
The idea that amounts should be recorded at the time they occur, not when cash is paid or received.

maturity
The end date of a contract.

merger
When two organizations come together to create one new company (verb: to merge).

minority interest
A shareholding of less than 50% in another company.

off-balance-sheet accounting
The structuring of certain transactions which might allow the company to leave large amounts out of the accounts.

parent company
A company which owns most of the shares in another company. (See also: subsidiary.)

provision
The inclusion in the accounts of amounts which may arise in the future.

prudence principle
The idea that financial information should be reported conservatively, so that it is not possible that the overall value of a company is overstated.

ratio
A mathematical calculation which compares one amount to another.

repair and maintenance
Costs to fix an asset (such as a machine), or the normal costs needed to keep the asset working properly.

salvage value
The estimated value of an asset at the end of its useful life.

scrap value
The sales value of an asset when it can no longer be used.

to service debt
To pay the interest and capital repayment in accordance with the loan contract.

stock
1) Another word for the shares of a company.
2) The inventory of a company, ie, the goods which have not been sold.

subsidiary
A company which is owned or controlled by another company. (See also: parent company.)

tax return
An official document sent to the tax authorities which states profit or loss, and is used to calculate how much tax has to be paid.

test basis
The process of checking a random sample of a list of items, to gain assurance that the complete list is correctly reported.

unrealized gain (loss)
The increase (decrease) in value of an asset which has not yet been sold.

Useful phrases and vocabulary

Meeting people

Hello, Mr/Ms ... . I'm ... .
It's nice to meet you.
– (It's) Nice to meet you, too.
May I introduce you to ... ?
I'd like to introduce you to ...
Have you met ... ?

Offering hospitality

Can I take your coat?
Please come in and take a seat.
Can I get you a cup of coffee/tea?
Would you like something to drink?
– Yes, please./Yes, that would be great.
– No, thank you./No, thanks.

Being polite (and less direct)

Excuse me, but ...
I'm sorry but ...
I'm afraid that's not quite right.
We have a slight problem.
At first glance, it appears clear ...
This seems to be ...
Could you please ... ?

Checking and clarifying information

Maybe you could clarify a couple of things.
– Sure./Certainly./How can I help?
What do these figures mean again?
– Basically, they just mean that ...
Can we just go over that one more time?
– Of course./No problem.
Could you repeat that, please?
– Sure, I said ...
You *did* say the 24th, didn't you?
– Yes, that's right.
I didn't quite catch that.
– OK, what I said was that ...
So, what you're saying is ...
– That's right./Exactly.
So, this column is wrong?
– Well, not exactly./It depends how you see it.
How is the profit calculated?
– Well, it's actually quite simple. First we ...
In other words, we'll need to send it by Friday?
– Exactly./Yes, if we want to meet the deadline.
How about if we send it in next week?
– That'll be fine./Oh, I'm sorry, that would be too late.

Talking about causes and results

Cause
This happened because ...
This (increase/decrease) is due to ...
This is a result of ...

Result
It could lead to ...
What could happen is ...
Because of this, we'll see ...

Talking about figures

Going up ↗
Figures have increased slightly.
Figures have increased steadily.
Figures have increased dramatically.
It's not as low as last year.
It's slightly/a lot more this year.
The situation was pretty bad, but is now improving
 slowly.
It's better than last year.
Profits rose/increased last year.

Going down ↘
This is a significant/gradual drop.
Profits have been falling/going down since the fire.
It's gone down/fallen since last year.
There's quite a drop from 2000 to 2001.

No change →
The situation is stable.
We're hovering at around 3%.
It's virtually/exactly the same.

Ups and downs ∧∧↘
There have been some fluctuations.

Telephone phrases

Getting through
Hello, this is ... from ... . May I speak to ... , please?
Could you put me through to ... ?
– Janet speaking.
Hello, Janet. It's Klaus.

Making appointments
Could you come by the office next week?
How/What about Monday at 9.30?
Can you make Tuesday afternoon?
– No, I'm sorry. I'm busy then.
– Yes, that sounds good.